Portrait of a
President

PORTRAIT BY ARNOLD NEWMAN COURTESY HOLIDAY

Portrait of a President

JOHN F. KENNEDY IN PROFILE

WILLIAM MANCHESTER

LITTLE, BROWN AND COMPANY · BOSTON · TORONTO

LIBRARY OF CONGRESS CATALOG CARD NO. 62–17959

Fourth Printing

Parts of this book first appeared in *Holiday*.

Published simultaneously in Canada
by Little, Brown & Company (Canada) Limited

PRINTED IN THE UNITED STATES OF AMERICA

To
John Kennerly Manchester
and
to his future

Contents

Author's Note

INAUGURAL DAY dawned bleak and cold, and as the morning wore on it grew glum. The preliminary ceremonies were lagging. Outside the Capitol, impatient spectators shivered, while inside, the President-Elect, sharing their mood, fingered his speech in the Military Affairs Committee Room. Ten minutes before noon he moved restlessly into the corridor, but he didn't get far; the Secretary of the Senate barred the way, explaining that the Upper House wasn't ready to receive him. "All right," the President-to-be said cheerfully. "We'll go back and wait some more."

That was almost three decades ago. The following morning — March 5, 1933 — a brief version of the episode was published on an inside page of the *New York Times*. Eight days later it appeared in *Time*, and there it was discovered in the 1950's by a Harvard professor preparing a multi-volume chronicle of the Roosevelt era. In itself the story is trivial, merely suggestive of Franklin Roosevelt's resilience. History, however, is a gossamer spun of such incidents, and the pilgrimage of this one, from a brittle page of newsprint to Arthur M. Schlesinger, Jr.'s *The Crisis of the Old Order*, tells a great deal about the spinner's trade. Reporters and scholars are inclined to think of themselves as antithetical. Call a newspaperman's copy recondite and he reaches for a pica ruler; tell a professor his paper is just journalism and he invites you to join him in the gym. The feud is an old one. It is time to stop it. The only difference between the two is a difference of time; today's journalism is tomorrow's history.

Portrait of a President is journalism. The writer has labored on the other side of the barricade, but this monograph has been written while moving along the advancing edge of the present. It is not definitive in any sense, nor does it pretend to be an assessment of the Kennedy Administration. Proximity to great events distorts our vision, and the few tentative judgments I have set down may be quickly outdated. The political tide has a way of washing away those who would predict its course. I freely concede, for example, that on the morning after the off-year elections I may devoutly wish that I could run a few pages through the typewriter once more, and in that context it may be useful to point out that the period of my study has been from April 1961 to April 1962 — roughly, from Cuba to Big Steel. Some may conclude from this that the text is a narrative, beginning with failure and ending in triumph. For them one more warning flag must be hoisted. This is not a chronological account. It is, rather, an attempt to understand and explain a highly complex individual playing a unique role. Thus its material is not confined to the year of investigation. I have, as it were, revved the film of John Kennedy's life through a series of projectors, stopping it whenever I found a relevant frame. The sum of these superimposed frames is, or is meant to be, something resembling a portrait.

Bibliognosts will note that there are few footnotes. Work of this sort cannot be annotated. Because so much of the material could only be attributed to what academics call "personal information," the writer would be constantly referring himself to himself — a pedagogic absurdity. Moreover, if every fact were subject to direct citation, the manuscript could not have been written. Readers will find that I revere the Presidency and admire this President; nevertheless, those who are close to a Chief Executive in office are not likely to deal with any writer, however sympathetic, who cannot shield them from embarrassment. Thus from time to time the text refers to "an aide," "an ex-roommate," "an adviser," etc. At present you have only my word that these people exist, although I have arranged to deposit my files in the Olin Library, Wesleyan University, Middletown, Connecticut.

My chief sources are personal observations of the President in 1961 and 1962 and some forty other interviews with members of his Administration, his family, his present friends, and those who have known him in the past. Whenever possible I have used my legs to track down data, but journalism, like history, is a ceaseless flow. Much that follows is a synthesis of my own findings and those of others. My debt to my colleagues is great and is gratefully acknowledged. Occasionally I encountered different versions of the facts; in those cases I settled for the account which seemed to me to be correct. Among the books which were especially helpful were *John Kennedy: A Political Profile,* by James MacGregor Burns (New York: Harcourt, Brace, 1960); *PT 109: John F. Kennedy in World War II,* by Robert J. Donovan (New York: McGraw-Hill, 1961); *Let Us Begin: The First 100 Days of the Kennedy Administration,* comprising contributions from Eric F. Goldman, Barbara Ward, Wallace Westfeldt, Jr., Ira Wolfert, Sidney Hyman, and Martin Agronsky (New York: Simon and Schuster, 1961); *The American President,* by Sidney Hyman (New York: Harper, 1954); *Why England Slept,* by John F. Kennedy (New York: Funk, 1940); *Profiles in Courage,* by John F. Kennedy (New York: Harper, 1936); *To Turn the Tide: A Selection from President Kennedy's Public Statements from His Election Through the 1961 Adjournment of Congress, Setting Forth the Goals of His First Legislative Year,* edited by John W. Gardner, with a foreword by Carl Sandburg and an introduction by President Kennedy (New York: Harper, 1962); *I'm for Roosevelt,* by Joseph P. Kennedy (New York: Reynal and Hitchcock, 1936); *The American Presidency: An Interpre-*

tation, by Harold J. Laski (New York: Harper, 1940); *The Remarkable Kennedys,* by Joseph P. McCarthy (New York: Dial, 1960); *Presidential Power: The Politics of Leadership,* by Richard Neustadt (New York: John Wiley, 1960); *Six Crises,* by Richard M. Nixon (New York: Doubleday, 1962); *The Kennedy Government,* by Stan Opotowsky (New York: E. P. Dutton, 1961); *Abraham Lincoln: The War Years,* Volume Four, by Carl Sandburg (New York: Harcourt, Brace, 1939); *The Crisis of the Old Order, 1919-1933,* by Arthur M. Schlesinger, Jr. (Boston: Houghton Mifflin, 1957); *The Coming of the New Deal,* also by Mr. Schlesinger (Boston: Houghton Mifflin, 1958); and *The Making of the President 1960,* by Theodore H. White (New York: Atheneum, 1961).

The number of newspaper and magazine sources on any Administration approaches infinity. During this inquiry I drew on the files of the *New York Times* — a very special debt — and on the Associated Press, the *Chicago Daily News,* the *Greensboro Daily News,* the *Hartford Courant,* the *Harvard Alumni Bulletin,* the *New York Herald Tribune,* the *New York Times Magazine, The Times* of London, United Press International, the *Wall Street Journal,* the *Washington Post and Times-Herald,* the *Department of State Bulletin, Esquire, Harper's Magazine, Holiday, Life, Look, Nation's Business,* the *New Republic, Newsweek,* the *New Yorker,* the *Reporter,* the *Saturday Evening Post,* the *Saturday Review, Time,* and *U.S.*

News and World Report. Signed articles that were particularly valuable include Stewart Alsop's "The White House Insiders," *Saturday Evening Post* (June 10, 1961); Russell Baker's "Why Kennedy Has Trouble on the Hill," *New York Times Magazine* (April 16, 1961); David Butler's "An Englishman's Reflections on the Change of Administration," *American Scholar* (Autumn, 1961); Douglass Cater's "The Kennedy Look in the Arts," *Horizon* (September, 1961); Frederic W. Collins's "The Mind of John F. Kennedy," *New Republic* (May 8, 1961); Rowland Evans, Jr.'s "That Wit in the White House," *Saturday Evening Post* (September 2, 1961); Arthur N. Holcombe's "John F. Kennedy '40 as Presidential Cabinet-Maker," *Harvard Alumni Bulletin* (May 27, 1961); Alfred Kazin's "The President and Other Intellectuals," *American Scholar* (Autumn, 1961); Fletcher Knebel's "Kennedy and His Pals," *Look* (April 25, 1961); Raymond Moley's "FDR — JFK: A Brain Truster Compares Two Presidents," *Newsweek* (April 17, 1961); Hans J. Morganthau's " 'Alone with Himself and History,' " *New York Times Magazine* (November 13, 1960); Richard H. Rovere's "Notes on the Establishment in America," *American Scholar* (Autumn, 1961); William V. Shannon's "The Kennedy Administration: The Early Months," *American Scholar* (Autumn, 1961), and the Washington dispatches of Joseph Alsop, Marquis Childs, Henry Gemill, Arthur Krock, Walter Lippmann, Allan L. Otten, James Reston, and Merriman Smith.

The writer offers deepest thanks to those individuals who gave generously of their time, provided advice, loaned material, and furnished their recollections of the past and their reflections on the present. Inevitably some names must be omitted, but special gratitude is extended to:

John F. Kennedy, President of the United States of America;

Mr. K. LeMoyne Billings; Professor and Mrs. James M. Burns; Miss Christine Camp; Mr. Douglass Cater; Mrs. Russell G. D'Oench; Mr. Paul B. Fay, Jr., Undersecretary of the Navy; Mr. Richard N. Goodwin, Assistant Secretary of State for Inter-American Affairs; Mr. Andrew T. Hatcher, Associate Press Secretary to the President; Mr. Cornelius W. Heine; Mr. Fred Holborn, Special Assistant to the President; Mr. Edward M. Kennedy; Mr. Joseph P. Kennedy; Mr. Robert F. Kennedy, Attorney General of the United States; Mr. Joseph P. Kirby; Mr. Arthur Krock; Mrs. Evelyn Lincoln, personal secretary to the President; Mr. Lawrence F. O'Brien, Special Assistant to the President; Mr. P. Kenneth O'Donnell, Special Assistant to the President; Mr. David Powers, Special Assistant to the President; Mr. James A. Reed, Assistant Secretary of the Treasury; Mr. George Ross; Mr. Pierre Salinger, Press Secretary to the President; Mr. Arthur M. Schlesinger, Jr., Special Assistant to the President; Mr. Harry Sions, Editorial Director of *Holiday Magazine;* Mr. Theodore C. Sorensen, Special Counsel to the President; Miss Pamela Turnure,

Press Secretary to Mrs. John F. Kennedy; and Mr. Gore Vidal.

The views in the text are not always their views, and certainly the responsibility for any sins of omission or commission is mine alone, but without their cooperation this study would have been impossible, and without the insight they have given me it would be a bloodless audit. Whatever its other faults, I hope that it is more than that.

W.M.

Middletown, Connecticut
May, 1962

ONE

You Must Never Forget

THE WHITE HOUSE is very white. Under a roving moon its freshly painted sandstone walls gleam through Andrew Jackson's beloved magnolias with a haunting, ghostcandle glow, and the barbered lawn lies quiet as a park, and sometimes, when the light shifts, the mansion seems to recede. Partly this is a trick of landscaping, partly it is us. So much intrudes. Americans take their Presidency personally. In retrospect you recall pledges of allegiance in chalkdusty classrooms, and blue eagles, and Hoover's medicine ball, and Raymond Massey in that odd hat, and Carl Sandburg writing of the day the calendar said Good Friday —

The oaks and chestnuts stood grave and thoughtful.

From any window of the honorable Executive Mansion they were above reproach. . . .

Did any clairvoyant foreteller write a forecast that today, this April the Fourteenth, one man must hear a deep sea bell and a farewell gong and take a ride skyward swifter than Elijah in the chariot of fire?

Thus mythbound, you lurk behind the old black iron fence on Pennsylvania Avenue, squinting at the floodlit north façade. The haze of tribal sentiment grows denser. You can scarcely believe that the shrine is inhabited.

It is, because the White House is also a house. The lower rooms lack domesticity — each year over a million tourists file through them under the illusion that they are seeing the President's lodgings, when all they are in is a museum — but when a concealed elevator rises to the second floor above ground level you emerge in the First Family's residential apartment, and there the tone is quite different. This suite is closed to the public; no part of it was shown on CBS's Jacqueline Kennedy Show. It is very much a home, though not all the public would recognize it as such, because it is so precisely upper-class. The last tenants were comfortably middle-class. Their tastes ran to the music of Fred Waring and Lawrence Welk; to color television sets, red leather chairs, war trophies. Today the only martial note among the furnishings is the photograph of the First Lady's father wearing a World War I second lieutenant's uniform, and even he gazes out from his frame with genteel, East Egg urbanity.

The new look is subdued elegance. Achieving it was no mean accomplishment. The mansion has changed enormously since the days when John G. Nicolay called it "a dirty, rickety concern," yet it can scarcely be called a triumph of design. Ceilings are lofty dustcatchers, rooms are chopped up, doors open inconveniently. Stepping from the elevator you find yourself in a small vestibule which debouches into a huge hall. This passage runs east and west, bisecting the entire floor like a concourse and creating something of a traffic problem. The President's oval study opens on it from the south, and so — directly across from the elevator — does his bedroom. The children sleep along the north side. The western extremity of the corridor has been converted into a family sitting room, which leads to the First Lady's bedroom and the dining room. This arrangement is successful, but eastward the yawning hall ends in splendid anticlimax. The state bedrooms are down there. In them, theoretically, eminent guests from other nations may retire to enjoy an enticing view of the Treasury next door. Actually celebrities board in Blair House, and the state rooms, always vacant, somehow evoke memories of a resort hotel out of season.

The effect could easily be that of a refurbished New York elevator flat. It's not, because the great, barnlike corridor has been toned down by an ingenious use of color, *objets d'art,* and graceful furniture. Slipcovered French chairs are grouped invitingly on off-white rugs. Lovely chandeliers sparkle overhead. American paintings by George Catlin, Maurice Prendergast, Winslow Homer, and John Singer Sargent hang on tinted walls, and below them are handsomely mounted vases and sculptures, a Louis Quinze desk, and a spinet. The most vivid hues, however, come from book jackets. Altogether there are several thousand volumes, rising in endless tiers: graceful books on art, squat histories, multi-volume encyclopedias, Churchill's memoirs, a few modern novels — Nevil Shute's *On the Beach,* Giuseppe di Lampedusa's *The Leopard,* Harper Lee's *To Kill a Mockingbird* — and many biographies, including a battered, jacketless copy of *Profiles in Courage,* which seems a shabby orphan here, because everything else is tidy and quietly expensive. The hi-fi-FM-TV in the west sitting room is long, low, masked. The portable bar there is stocked with Beefeater gin and Ballantine's Scotch ("She hath done what she could," read the fatalistic banner which the W.C.T.U. gave the mansion in memory of Mrs. Rutherford B. "Lemonade Lucy" Hayes). White matchbooks bear the gold inscription *The President's House,* and the spine of a buckram scrapbook the simple legend *Caroline.*

Caroline's father approaches with celerity, shoulders hunched and burnished black shoes gliding in a Boston social gait. His dress conforms to the décor: a tailored two-button navy blue suit, a white shirt with a spread collar, a narrow Ivy tie held by a gold alligator-grip clasp shaped like a tiny PT boat. Like many public men he seems shorter than his photographs, and startlingly older. On television he looks younger than his age, but forty million screens are wrong. The figure tapers like a boxer's; the glossy hair is chestnut, with only a suggestion of gray at the temples. The face, however, is deeply lined, especially around the mouth, and the eyes give an even stronger impression of maturity. They are opaque, gray, and often hooded by long lashes. There is about them an air of being withdrawn, as John Hay wrote of Lincoln, into "an inner sanctuary of thought, sitting in judgment on the scene and feeling its far reach into the future." It is impossible to read John Fitzgerald Francis Kennedy's mind, but obviously there is much on it. Upon the evening of this visit he has been President of the United States nearly a year.

"Let's go in here." (The familiar, starchy *he-ah.*) He moves past his bedroom door, toward the formal, yellow-walled oval study which looks out on the Washington Monument, and opening the door he precedes his visitor. This is protocol. Over four hundred indignant letters have inquired of the White House why the President always seems to be a few steps ahead of his wife. "Jackie," he once replied lightly, "will just have to walk faster." Actually she's not allowed to. The President outranks everyone, including ladies. On Cape Cod, or in Virginia or Florida, Jacqueline goes first at his insistence, but in the capital that's out. Early in his administration he tried to hold a door for Eleanor Roosevelt. She hung back.

"No, you go first," she said. "You are the President."

He laughed. "I keep forgetting."

"But you must never forget," Mrs. Roosevelt said gently.

He remembers now. We sit in the study — he in his upholstered Northern Porch rocker, a duplicate of the one downstairs in his West Wing office — and he reflects on the changes which the Presidency has wrought in his life.

"In eleven weeks I went from senator to President, and in that short space of time I inherited Laos, Cuba, Berlin, the nuclear threat, and all the rest. It was a terrific adjustment to make. I've made it now, but naturally there have been some changes. It's certainly true that I'm more isolated socially. In the beginning I tried to carry on the life I had led, going out, seeing people; but I soon realized that was impossible. Apart from state dinners I suppose I see only three or four people socially. But I have no feeling of withdrawing. After all, everyone's life is circumscribed. And in many ways I see and hear more than anyone else."

His right hand, which is never still — it almost seems to have a life of its own — drums on a matchbook, on the rocker arm, on a shaving scar, on his teeth. His eyes are hooded. For a long moment the only sounds are the rhythmic rock of the chair and the muted tick of a gold mantel clock behind him.

Then:

"So much depends on my actions. So I am seeing fewer people, simplifying my life, organizing it so that I am not always on the edge of irritability."

The hand makes a sudden, spastic fist.

Talking with writers is one of the President's relaxations, and presently he does relax, speaking with clarity and wit about his early life, his family, the war years, the years in Congress, and his rise to the most powerful office in the world. It is a pleasant evening. Yet beneath us the oaks and chestnuts stand grave and thoughtful. Every hour in the Executive Mansion is an hour in history. In South Vietnam tonight Communist guerrillas are attacking in battalion strength. In Algeria one O.A.S. threatens a putsch, while in South America another O.A.S. quibbles over Cuban sanctions. Andrei Gromyko is insisting that East Germans be given full control over Berlin access routes. London feels bullish about a new summit, Paris is grimly bearish, and Syria is seething. At home Jimmy Hoffa is celebrating his fourth anniversary as Teamster president, while the Senate Armed Services

Committee has announced that it will hold hearings on Administration censorship of Pentagon brass Housing, unemployment, and gold — each a code word for a knotty problem — have a brighter sound these days, thanks to vigorous executive action. There is still a ten per cent gap between the nation's productive capacity and its actual performance, however, and even the educators seem uninterested in education. The country as a whole feels sanguine but there are many dissidents. Alfred Kazin is uneasy. Dwight Eisenhower is unhappy; so, even at this early date, is Roger M. Blough. The Americans for Democratic Action are most unhappy, and Margaret Chase Smith wonders aloud whether the author of *Profiles* lacks the courage to blow up the world.

Instinctively all these — and Gromyko, Macmillan, de Gaulle, and even Hoffa — turn to 1600 Pennsylvania Avenue. It is the one place to which every buck is passed and where, as Harry Truman observed, the buck stops. Early in his tenure Kennedy had an imperfect understanding of this. At meetings of the National Security Council he would inquire of issues, "Let's see — did we inherit these, or are they our own?" It was Douglas MacArthur, of all people, who reminded him that the Presidency is a continuum. "The chickens are coming home to roost," the fading old soldier told him, "and you live in the chicken house." Ultimately every American problem becomes the President's. At the same time, the number of issues has multiplied. Because the world is more comlex, and because this nation plays a larger role in it, he Chief Executive is empowered to make command decisions that were inconceivable twenty years igo, which means that Senator Smith's speech — whatever one thinks of her discretion — was directed to the right address.

To this address, to this home, and to its householder. The President must never forget, nor can he. More and more the discussion with his evening visitor turns to Germany, South America, domestic legislation, and the Soviet position on arms control, a problem so renitent that young John Kennedy analyzed it in his undergraduate thesis two decades ago. These quarters are *en famille*, but public life is never truly private once an ivory Princess telephone across the room rings. If a matter is urgent, any one of several aides or Cabinet ministers may call him at any hour. And once, as we stand by the blue and gold presidential flag, looking out at the winking red lights of the bone-white Monument, the President speaks of his Hairbreadth Harry mandate. "I've gone over the election hurdle," he says, his hand exploring in his hair. "Now I have the necessary support at home. This — this *base* is all-important. A chief of state cannot deal abroad effectively unless he has it. I'm over the hump now, but the first four months were delicate."

The early days of any Administration are vital, in the opinion of Columbia Professor Richard E. Neustadt, whose scholarly volume *Presidential Power* John Kennedy read during the 1960 campaign. Neustadt wrote that a Chief Executive's public image "takes shape for most constituents no later than the first time they see him being President (a different thing from seeing him as a candidate)." The first time Kennedy's constituents saw him as President he was at the post and pulling away. Noticing that there were no Negroes among the Coast Guard cadets in the inaugural parade, he started an official inquiry on the spot. The next morning he was in his bare office, witnessing the swearing in of his Cabinet, pumping Harry Truman's hand, and firing off Executive Order No. 1, to double the food rations of four million needy Americans. In the weeks which followed he continued to vibrate with energy. He would pace corridors, read on his feet, dictate rapidly, dart out for brisk constitutionals around the monument, and return in a sprint, snapping his restless fingers. "I never heard of a President who wanted to know so much," said Charles Bohlen. Some members of the government were so hard-pressed by the President that routine work suffered. A committee chairman from the Hill complained, "*He* may have two hours to spend, but *I* don't"; and Llewellyn Thompson, Ambassador to Russia, who was seldom alone with Eisenhower for more than ten minutes, had four two-hour sessions with Kennedy. The talk wasn't small talk. "When you see the President," a senator remarked, "you have to get in your car and drive like blazes back to the Capitol to beat his memo commenting on what you told him."

One day a hundred people were counted entering the West Wing office. One powwow there produced seventeen separate directives, and two months after taking the oath the new Chief Magistrate had issued thirty-two official messages and legislative recommendations — Eisenhower had issued five in his first two months — while delivering twelve speeches, promulgating twenty-two Executive Orders and proclamations, sending twenty-eight communications to foreign chiefs of state, and holding seven press conferences. A Washington wag observed that the new President seemed determined to be not only his own Secretary of State, but his own Mrs. Roosevelt, too. No detail seemed too small for him. Noting that Army guerrillas had been deprived of their green berets, he ordered that they be returned. Conferring with generals about Southeast Asian strategy, he tested the carbines being shipped to Saigon, and as his first presidential spring approached he even detected crab grass on the greening White House lawn and told the gardeners to get rid of it.

Some of his early activity was an extension of the inaugural binge: being President was fun. Some of it was a carryover from three years of incessant barnstorming: he was still behaving like a nominee. And some was a natural consequence of his appetite for work. Both John and Bobby Kennedy had spent most of their Washington years toiling at the other end of

Pennsylvania Avenue; they were genuinely amazed
to learn that all executive offices shut down Saturdays.
The Attorney General sent a note of appreciation to
everyone who had worked in the Justice Building
on the Administration's first Washington's Birthday,
and the President ordered Saturday office hours for
his staff to set a good (if vain) example for the rest of
the government.

But the hatless, coatless, on-the-ball vigor also had
a shrewd political motive. Kennedy was out to ex-
pand that all-important base. The people he needed
were watching him, and he wanted to be sure they
liked what they saw. Americans approve of self-
starters. Thus it was helpful for reporters to report
that the new President was very much in charge and
was encumbered by piles of documents and swarms of
advisers; useful for the word to be passed that Dean
Acheson had been given just four days to hammer out
a detailed NATO report. The first, televised press
conferences were, of course, crucial. One of them —
the third — was watched by some sixty-five million
people in twenty-one and a half million homes. These
performances were live. Kennedy had to be not only
his own Mrs. Roosevelt, but also his own Robert
Montgomery. Bearing down in his best IBM manner,
he became something of his own Mnemosyne as well;
reporters learned that the President knew all about
the sale of a surplus Navy building in West Virginia
and could quote from memory a statistic about Cu-

ban molasses which had appeared four days earlier near the end of a government report.

The wisdom of the Neustadt approach was presently reflected in studies by opinion samplers. Kennedy's racing start had converted a quarter of the American electorate. His base was as big as Ike's. And in the quiet of his study he concedes that this effect was calculated: "I've always believed that a first impression is important. In press conferences I gave the impression of knowing what I was doing, and my general activity, in my judgment, stimulated confidence. Cuba could have been difficult if I hadn't done that."

"Presidents, like great French restaurants, have an *ambiance* all their own," Douglass Cater has observed. The Kennedy image was forming, an amalgam of Jacqueline's camellia beauty, Caroline's Kate Greenaway charm, the Ciceronian rhetoric of the President's speeches, the football on the Attorney General's desk, the generous gestures toward the defeated party, and the new idealism. Gone were the Mad Avenue slogans ("bigger bang for a buck," "rolling readjustment," "brinksmanship," "agonizing reappraisal"); instead there was to be a policy of action, typified by the new Secretary of Labor, who settled a strike during his first twenty-four hours in office and announced that in the new Washington the deadline for everything would be "the day before yesterday." Like the harassed senator, everyone in the new Cabinet appeared to be driving like blazes, working fourteen-hour days and displaying symptoms of Kennedy hypomania. *He* One was observed simultaneously signing his mail, carrying on a telephone conversation, and relaying instructions to his secretary by crude semaphore; a second barely found time to take his own oath of office; and a third, Robert McNamara, startled Pentagon guards by his habit of showing up at 7:30 each morning, his ballpoint at the ready.

Today the Administration looks back wistfully on its first flush of enthusiasm. There was a freshness then, a boundless vitality; and perhaps there was also some naïveté. "We had the feeling that there was a plasticity to events, that they could be molded, that this guy was unlimited," Special Assistant Arthur M. Schlesinger, Jr., recalls. John Kennedy seemed to share that feeling. After the inaugural parade he had reached the White House in a state of euphoria. "He was exalted," says Ted Sorensen, Special Counsel to the President. "It was no secret that he wanted the Presidency. He had won it in a bitter contest. Like most men he was ambitious in his profession, and now he was at the pinnacle."

Any man who reaches that pinnacle brings a gang with him. Schlesinger and Sorensen were typical of Kennedy's. The capital was enchanted by the invasion of a witty, bespectacled delegation of ideologues, most of them with advanced degrees, all of which seemed to have been granted in Cambridge, Massachusetts. "If you think Republicans are lonely in

Washington," said Senator Thruston B. Morton, "you ought to be a Yale Republican." "The definition of a failure," one of the arrivals' bright flashes went, "is a Yale man driving an Edsel with a Nixon sticker on it." They might have said an *old* Yale man. For the incomers were much younger than the outgoers, and it is significant that their first inspiration, the Peace Corps, was an appeal to young bloods.

"The torch," the President had said on the Capitol steps, "has been passed to a new generation of Americans." Walter Lippmann reckoned the difference between the Eisenhower and Kennedy Administrations at about thirty years, and to venerable Washingtonians the junior members of the new team seem very junior indeed. During Eisenhower's first inauguration Sorensen was an angry young man of the A.D.A. Jacqueline Bouvier was a giddy girl interviewing inaugural celebrities; as Madame de Gaulle's guest in 1961 she still looked rather like a *jeune fille* traveling under the eagle eye of her chaperone. Bobby Kennedy's wife Ethel refers to politicos as "goodies" and "baddies." It is startling to recall that when John Kennedy first ran against the baddies in 1946, Ethel's husband was too young to do more than work the streets of Cambridge under the supervision of Le-Moyne Billings, who had roomed with the candidate at Choate School. At the time of the Berlin airlift the present Attorney General was a cub reporter for the now defunct Boston *Post*, and five years later, when working for Senator Joseph McCarthy, he was able to slip undetected into a football game between Harvard and Yale dormitory teams. Senator John L. McClellan continues to treat him with a paternalistic air, even as, in the first days of the New Frontier, the United States Ambassador to the United Nations was fatherly toward the President of the United States. Twice in the Administration's first year — during the Cuban episode and the Freedom Rides — Yale graduates ran afoul of Harvard men. Each clash had overtones of The Game. In the first, Richard Bissell of the CIA and the Blue seemed to some to be a scapegoat for the Crimson. In the second, the Attorney General argued with a group of Riders from New Haven, one of whom alleges that the President's brother called them "a bunch of Yalies."

This collegiate theme is both entertaining and deceptive. John Kennedy may be "the boy" to Eisenhower, but at forty-five he has his full growth. His is the youngest Cabinet since McKinley's, but George Washington's was younger than either. Despite G.O.P wheezes about the children's crusade, most of the Administration's movers and shakers are middle-aged, and they have the diversity of mature men. Niccolò Machiavelli, who preceded Neustadt, believed that "the first impression that one gets of a ruler and of his brains is from seeing the men he has around him." Anyone who takes a sharp look at the men around Kennedy discovers that the genus falls into three distinct species: the professors (Rooseveltians); the politicians (chiefly Irish); and such old friends as Lem Billings and Charles F. Spalding, a New York investment banker. Each group has its own traits. The old friends have known the President longest. Unlike Eisenhower, whose presidential friendships were formed late in life, Kennedy has been close to most of these men for at least twenty years. Collectively they are trustworthy, loyal, helpful, friendly mesomorphs. They are well-heeled and often Republicans, though it would be wrong to underscore that, because they never argue about politics. The professors, on the other hand, argue about politics all the time, while the Irish politicians listen to your arguments and then agree warmly, because they are empathic, flexible, and lacking in the self-consciousness of the intellectuals. When Secretary of Commerce Luther Hodges was Governor of North Carolina, he posed for a national magazine in shorts stamped *Made in N.C.* Professor Schlesinger and Dean McGeorge Bundy never appear publicly in their underwear.

Hodges is over sixty. In a government whose average minister is in his forties, this places him, chronologically at least, beyond the New Frontier. It also puts him outside the circle of presidential intimates, the most prominent members of which are the Attorney General, thirty-five, Robert McNamara, forty-five, Douglas Dillon, fifty-two, and Arthur Goldberg, fifty-three, of the Cabinet; Appointments Secretary Ken O'Donnell, thirty-eight, in whom the President places great trust; Schlesinger, forty-four, to whom he likes to talk; and Bundy, forty-three, and Sorensen, thirty-three, the two advisers who exert the greatest influence on him. Thus, while this is not an Administration of yearlings, some grasp of the generational factor is essential to an understanding of the Kennedy Presidency. The fact that the Chief Executive has surrounded himself with contemporaries suggests its importance to him, and it has loomed large in his career. The anybody-but-Jack coalition which formed before his nomination was really a bloc of older men fighting younger men. Behind the charge of Kennedy "inexperience" lay the resentment of old stagers who were being shoved into the wings, and behind the urbane manners of the Frontiersmen today there is a similar awareness of age.

This is the veteran generation. They were young in the early 1940's, and most of them were very much in the war. Men Eisenhower's age were in charge of the maps, but men Kennedy's age did the actual fighting. The President himself was a PT commander in the Solomon Islands. A fellow officer — who laid his hand open while operating one of the boat's machine guns — was Lieutenant (j.g.) Byron R. White, now Mr. Justice White. On nearby Bougainville, Orville Freeman, the present Secretary of Agriculture, was a Marine officer; his face still bears scars of a Japanese bullet. Ken O'Donnell was a fighter pilot, Schlesinger was in the OSS, Press Secretary Pierre Salinger was a teen-age minesweeper captain. Even Robert Kennedy enlisted in the Navy at the age of seventeen, though he missed combat, which annoyed him no end. Afterward he went to South America with Lem Billings. "The war was still fresh in people's minds down there," Billings recalls, "and they'd ask where we had been, what we'd done. Bobby didn't have anything to say. I used to kid him about it. He didn't think it especially funny."

The thought of Bobby at war is diverting — he is warlike enough in peacetime — but his intuition was correct. He had missed the central, formative episode of his time. The style of the Frontier was shaped in those years. When John Kennedy was asked about his reaction to F.D.R.'s death in 1945 he replied calmly, "I had no deeply traumatic experience." This may puzzle those who remember the grief among civilians. It is less surprising to men who spent the early Forties on the red, ragged fringe of the war; they had learned to keep themselves to themselves, to avoid getting hurt. Today the President, speaking in the idiom of his time, scorns soul-searching as "couch talk," and nearly all those who are close to him hold the world at arm's length. There is no Adlai Stevenson among them; eloquence is not their forte. Their strong points are manipulation, expertise, and efficiency, even to the sacrifice of individuality. "We're developing a new policy community here," one of the Harvard men says. "Most of the men around Kennedy are not only of the same generation; they're alike in other ways, too. They all went to college, they're political creatures — though none are stridently political — and they have pretty much the same gifts. The fact that they have different titles is just accident, and they know it. People like Bohlen, Nitze, Bundy, and Rostow could easily have one another's jobs. You might say they're interchangeable parts."

Since age seems to attract the President more than party labels — Bundy, Dillon, and McNamara are Republicans — this writer suggested that he is a generational chauvinist. "I don't think that's the right word," he said reflectively. "I suppose that if you went through my Administration you'd find that most of my advisers are my age, give or take eight years. But I think most people are more comfortable with people their own age." They are, though few are as devoted to their peer group as he is. His partiality is clearly a factor in his personal diplomacy; he is proud of his relationships with Konrad Adenauer and Harold Macmillan, yet he has seemed more at ease with Hugh Gaitskell and Willy Brandt. Charles de Gaulle is an exception to this rule. De Gaulle appears to belong not merely to a different generation, but to another century; he won't even have a telephone in his office. The President admires him, however, and he made elaborate preparations for their first meeting. "It went off beautifully," one of the men who was present says trenchantly. "De Gaulle was like a professor. Our man was the student who had boned up. We got A."

The old guard does die, of course. Observing Bobby's whirlwind activity in Tokyo, a septuagenarian Japanese politician sighed, "The days are here for the younger generation to take over." Lippmann once noted that about fifteen years after every major war (*e.g.*, 1933) the wartime leaders reach senescence and political upheaval follows. John Kennedy feels that 1960 was an omen — that his generation is rising to power in other countries — and he has remarked more than once that by the time he leaves office he will probably be the senior statesman of the West. The change may brighten chances of understanding abroad, though it doesn't promise much on the Hill, where seniority assures a superannuated leadership. Roosevelt was thwarted by nine old men. Kennedy must deal with a Congress full of them.

The President's youthful informality is one of the sources of his political charm. In the Senate he had kept his office door open at all times, and it was after the inaugural, when his instincts were still those of the candidate, that he attempted "to carry on the life I had led." It was a plucky try, if soon abandoned. Unlike Bobby, he didn't work in his shirtsleeves. Away from his desk, however, he thought he needn't stand on ceremony. One evening he slipped into a neighborhood movie with a friend, Paul B. "Red" Fay, Jr., to see *Spartacus,* and one Saturday he picked up his golf clubs and completely vanished for three hours while the White House press corps seethed. He and Jacqueline also decided to go visiting like any other Washington couple. Here informality collided with the formality of the Presidency. Where a Chief Executive breaks bread, and who breaks it with him, is a matter of more than passing interest to the capital. Mainly it is the professional concern of twenty-four men in the Office of Protocol. Among other things there is a tradition that the occupant of the White House must remain socially aloof. As Herbert Hoover put it, "the President of the United States never calls on anyone." Precedent requires that the man who has solemnly sworn to execute the office of Chief Magistrate not only preserve, protect, and defend the Constitution, but that he do it, whenever possible, in his own home.

The First Family's hosts were to include Rowland Evans, Jr., of the New York *Herald Tribune*. Evans had told no one about it, not even his bureau chief. But in Washington there is a rather large number of people whose business it is to know the little preferences of a President — as, for example, the fact that John Kennedy's only cocktail is a daiquiri. Thus when the hostess phoned a Georgetown liquor dealer and emphatically ordered "one of your best bottles of rum," she told him more than she intended. "Why, Mrs. *Evans!*" he gasped. The secret was out. The morning of the party an Evans neighbor opened his front door and found his sidewalk encased in ice. Ice, however, was rapidly disappearing from the Evans walk; a small army of District employees was chipping away the last slivers. The neighbor asked huffily why the special treatment. He was told and since he, like Evans, was a member of the working press, the dream of a quiet evening out was destroyed. The workmen might as well have stuck around to render "Hail to the Chief."

The Chief hasn't retreated behind his seal. In many ways he is as informal as ever. Since the anniversary of his first year in office he has, some think, returned to his inaugural mood. Several friendships which had been interrupted have been renewed. In press conferences he is more relaxed, more buoyant — and, unfortunately, more likely to lapse into the spongy chaos of Eisenhower syntax. With an interviewer he continues to be as frank as Saint Augustine, and he still worries the Secret Service by falling into crowds and confounds Press Secretary Pierre Salinger by permitting him to distribute advance texts of presidential speeches which are then scrapped at the point of declamation. In Palm Beach or on Cape Cod, where, Bobby says, "he can really relax," he slips away now and then. A letter arrived from a Hyannis Port neighbor thanking him so much for calling; the billet created an anxious stir in the White House because, it developed, no one there had heard of the signer.

He has even made a few social sallies near the capital. Sargent Shriver, Director of the Peace Corps and his brother-in-law, was entertaining some eighty people late in Kennedy's second presidential winter when the door opened, admitting both the President *and* the Vice President. The guests, stunned, fell silent. Kennedy, prepared for this, moved about skill-fully, chatting until the party resumed its momentum. "It's a gift," observes Arthur Krock of the New York *Times*. "He doesn't know how to be stuffy." Occasion-ally his lack of stuffiness can result in wild incongru-ity. Once this writer was leaving the oval office in the West Wing. As he prepared to thread his way out through the maze of check points, Secret Service men, and White House police, the President said lightly, "Any time you're coming by, drop in."

Despite this casual air, his way of life has changed perceptibly since his investiture. He sees his films in a private theater under the mansion's East Terrace, where he laughed at *Make Mine Mink*, or in his father's projection room at the family compound on the Cape, where he tensely watched the demolition of *The Guns of Navarone*. He has always been an ar-dent movie-goer. Theaters have been his favorite form of election night relaxation; he took his grand-father to one when returns were being counted in his first primary, and went to another with two friends during the tense West Virginia primary of 1960. His all-time favorite is *Casablanca*, which he has seen at least four times, though while squiring Jacqueline Bouvier about he often took her to Westerns and Civil War pictures. During his first months in office he con-tinued to watch one or two films a week. Later the number dwindled; during a two-month period at the end of his first year in office he saw just five (*Paris Blues, Lover Come Back, Purple Hills, Carry on Con-*

stable, and *Loss of Innocence*). He has also become less patient with the screen. Before the inaugural he would sit through almost any flop. No more: if he becomes bored he may order that the last reel be shown, so he can see how everything turned out, or leave without a word. Since his election he has walked out on Elizabeth Taylor (*Butterfield 8*) and Marilyn Monroe (*The Misfits*), and he gave up on Billy Wilder's comedy *One, Two, Three,* perhaps because he can't see anything funny about Berlin.

So many topics are grave to a Chief Executive, and even if he tried to forget, he couldn't. Everyone he meets or knows is conscious of his office. The day after he defeated Richard Nixon in the wards of South Chicago a bunch of Kennedys were horsing around on the playing fields of Hyannis Port, watched by their peppery, seventy-two-year-old father, former Ambassador to Britain Joseph P. Kennedy, who is still known as "the ambassador." The President-Elect lunged at a long pass and missed, and the future Attorney General, on the other team, delivered an opinion. "All guts and no brains," he muttered lugubriously. Those present remember that, because they all knew it was the end of something. In the future such a razz would be disrespectful. The great days of touch were over; the new game was follow-the-leader. The same day several Kennedy friends were sitting in Bobby's Cape home when the leader entered, and they rose instinctively.

They didn't decide this, nor did he. Like his social

life, it was a matter of precedent. Something about the Presidency discourages familiarity; Schlesinger was once observed slipping into his suit coat before taking a telephone call from the oval office. That was a tribute, not to a man, but to an institution. The incumbent and the office reign together, which is why a Chief Executive speaks of himself, on formal occasions, as "we." Each inaugural brings renewed appreciation of this dualism. In 1932 the ambassador was traveling on Franklin Roosevelt's campaign train. After one of the candidate's speeches he accosted him with a blistering critique. "The stupidest thing I ever heard," he called it, adding a string of bitter epithets. Calling on President Roosevelt a few months later at the White House, he remembered that philippic. "I was appalled," he recalled recently. "It had been permissible then. But in the presence of the power and majesty of the Presidency it seemed unforgivable." George "Barney" Ross was similarly appalled when, upon being shown into President Kennedy's office, he blurted out, "Hi, Jack!" "I was mortified," Ross says. "I still brood over it. I'm not the kind that's disrespectful normally; it just popped out." Yet if anyone is entitled to be familiar with John Kennedy, it is Ross; as fellow officers they were shipwrecked together for five days during the war.

John Kennedy's age makes him a striking example of the power of custom. One afternoon in the White House this writer heard the bark of his voice approaching and heard, almost simultaneously, the rustle of expensive tweed. A few feet away Averell Harriman, a party power when John Kennedy was gyrating through the Big Apple in Harvard's Winthrop House, was coming to attention. Until his inaugural oath the President was still a junior senator. Yet men like Byrd, Keating, Eastland, and Dirksen defer to him now. "I haven't forfeited my faith in John Fitzgerald Kennedy!" the Republican Senate leader cried during the U.N. bond debate, while Carl Hayden, in his eighties, says simply, "I'm just anxious to be as helpful as I can to the President." Lyndon Johnson, who was Senator Kennedy's congressional leader and his chief rival for the 1960 nomination, has become almost unctuous. The President has described their new relationship as "a real love affair." "Lyndon has undergone a real metamorphosis," says a man who knows him well. "He used to be brisk, incisive. Now he dotes on Kennedy. He has become a rather sweet old man."

Today none of the Hyannis Port scrimmagers publicly use the President's first name in his presence. Bobby (to his chagrin) has remained Bobby — even in Cabinet meetings the Chief Executive so addresses him. Jack, however, has gone forever — in the same meetings, Bobby calls his brother "Mr. President." Only in private does the Attorney General revert to the diminutive, which in his case is "Johnny." Occasionally a show-off Boston pal writes a letter beginning "Dear Jack," but nearly everyone else is scrupulously correct. "I'm certainly not going to call my son 'Mr. President' when we're alone together," the ambassador remarked shortly before his stroke in December 1961, "but if there are people around we don't know very well I do, and it doesn't seem at all strange." "Jacqueline always calls him 'the President,'" says Arthur Krock, a friend of both since they were children. "She even calls him 'the President' to me." "I used to kid him all the time," says Red Fay, who, like Ross, served in the Navy with him, "but not any more. You just don't kid the President of the United States."

Once you did. Reportedly John Quincy Adams was subjected to a humiliating interview when a newspaperwoman discovered him swimming naked in the Potomac, sat on his clothes, and declined to leave until he had replied to her inquiries. Washingtonians of a century ago saw nothing remarkable in a Chief Executive insisting, "Call me Mr. Lincoln; 'Mr. President' is entirely too formal for us." Lincoln put up with extraordinary incivilities from strangers, but that was before the evolution of what Senator Eugene J. McCarthy has called the "cult of the Presidency." The cult has arisen because the President has become so much more sovereign. With the historic drift of power from Capitol Hill, more and more power has been vested in him. A few years ago the Hoover Commission found that among other things he was accountable for nine major departments, 104 bureaus, twelve sections, 108 services, fifty-one branches, 631 divisions, nineteen administrations, six agencies, four boards, six commands, twenty commissions, nineteen corporations, ten headquarters, three authorities, and 263 miscellaneous organizations. Since that survey his responsibilities have continued to multiply. No wonder we sir him, rise for him, and stand aside for him.

Thus the President is honored — and isolated. There is nothing teamy about the institution. It is no place for Groupthink. As a historian Kennedy knew that, but reality was still something of a blow. He had regarded political campaigning — "the treadmill," he calls it — as the most exhausting drudgery conceivable, and he has been startled to find that the Presidency is as demanding as it is. Those closest to him agree that it has affected him. Always introspective, he has, some feel, become readier to reveal his thoughts. During the worst of the Berlin crisis he phoned Fay. "Have you built your bomb shelter?" he inquired. "No, I built a swimming pool instead," Fay replied. "You made a mistake," the President commented. "And," Fay adds, "he was dead serious." The Attorney General thinks the fact that his brother has always been pensive means that he is less alone than most Chief Executives, though Bobby adds, "It's obvious that the possibilities of nuclear war are never far from his mind." In one of those bursts of frankness which startle writers the President told one of them, "If you could think only of yourself it would be easy to say you'd press the button, and easy to press it, too." That was after his somber Vienna meeting with

Khrushchev, when he asked his aides for an estimate of how many Americans might die in a nuclear holocaust. The answer was seventy million. It took a while to sink in. "He campaigned as a Democrat, and I don't think he fully understood what it meant to be President of all the people until after Vienna," a Republican friend observes. "Then he grasped, *really* grasped that the life of every man, woman, and child in this country — not to mention lives abroad — depended upon him." The President estimates that eighty per cent of his first year in office was spent mulling over foreign policy. In the 1960's foreign policy thoughts are long thoughts. "Of course he's preoccupied," a member of the Kennedy family remarks. "It would be a miracle if he weren't. Saigon, Germany, fifty-megaton bombs — that's why he can't get to sleep until two or three in the morning."

One worry which vexes him less is his image; he wears his political hat a bit more blithely. His skin is still thinner than that of most politicians, as witness his testy cancellation of all White House subscriptions to the New York *Herald Tribune*. Washington bureau chiefs have grown accustomed to phone calls from the President, and occasionally he boils over. Doris Fleeson, the liberal columnist, can make him growl; a *Fortune* harpoon drew presidential blood, and when Pauline Frederick appeared on NBC's Huntley-Brinkley Report to dispraise one of his U.N. decisions, he thundered right back at his television screen. Yet on the whole he seems quicker to shrug off press criticism than he was during his first weeks in the mansion. He is less vulnerable to such gadflies as David Lawrence, and as a rule he doesn't darken unless he thinks a critic has his facts balled up. A man can respond to just so many stimuli. A President has to be selective; he is likelier to survive if he remains in good spirits. Kennedy has become quicker to see, or even make, a joke at his own expense. In the Big Steel row he displayed a glint of humor, and during one of the councils of war over Cuba he listened quietly as speaker after speaker commented on the scope of the disaster; then, observing that the politicians looked desolate, he turned to Schlesinger and said dryly, "Arthur, when you write the history of my first term — *The Only Years* . . ."

Of course, he doesn't want them to be the only years. When eight-year-old Eric Sorensen wrote him that he liked the White House, the President wrote back, "So do I," and when Eric commented that he would enjoy living there some day, the presidential reply was, "Sorry, Eric, you'll have to wait your turn." The inaugural thrill has gone; each day he must make some thirty major decisions, and each decision leaves him with an endless agenda of unfinished business, but he seems to look forward confidently, and with relish, to a second term. Janio Quadros's resignation from the presidency of Brazil appalled him. "He doesn't have the right to resign!" he protested to a friend of the family who was with him at the time. "Sure, there are times when I'd like to go off to the

South of France and take in the sun, but no man can just quit his responsibilities and walk away." Even the desire to walk away is unlike him. His whole life has been a hunt for challenges. When he decided to stalk the Presidency, his father was dubious. "I said, 'What do you want that job for?'" Joe Kennedy recalled after the election. "I told him, 'It's the worst job in the world.' And he said, 'We've had problems for the past two thousand years, and they've been solved by humans, and today's can be, too.'" The ambassador's son had confidence in a specific human, himself. He retains it, though the first big rumble of his first term did inspire an agonizing reappraisal of some other bipeds across the river and under the trees of the Pentagon.

The Bay of Pigs was for him an hour of bitter truth. Its lessons are never far from his mind. In his first reaction to Quadros's charge that the Brazilian government had been undermined by foreign influences the President snapped, "If there was one place where we played it —" and he paused, "*straight* — it was in Brazil." In that pause he may have been thinking of Cuba. Cuba was not so straight. It was more of a sort of a three-cushion shot. Its failure to drop into the bag staggered the new President. "This is the first time he lost anything," an aide said. That fall he himself remarked that "If a man stays in hot politics long enough, he acquires an albatross," and Pig Bay, he added, was his. The implications of the tragedy were vast — they are still being discussed in the White

House, where Cuba is called "the bone in Kennedy's throat"—and among them was the realization that men thought to be infallible had proved to be highly fallible. "He had expected to rely on certain experts one hundred per cent," a presidential assistant explained, "and in this Cuban thing they let him down two hundred per cent." One Kennedy adviser stopped referring to the CIA at all. Instead he spoke scornfully of "the spies." "I know that outfit," said the ambassador, who was one of Eisenhower's intelligence advisers, "and I wouldn't pay them a hundred bucks a week. It's a lucky thing they were found out early; the best thing that could've happened, in fact. Cuba gave this Administration a chance to be great."

Certainly Washington's mood changed sharply. The football disappeared from Bobby's desk; his brother became more difficult to see. Their first-stage rocket had burned out. It was time a new guidance system took over. "We were like a gambler whose winning streak has been broken," says one of the young Cantabs. "Laos came at the same time, and then Berlin. The world appeared more intractable." The Bay of Pigs adventure had been so disastrous that a repetition was unthinkable. Immediate solutions were elusive, yet all problems were urgent, and growing more so. "Every incoming American Administration plunges at once into international crisis," Barbara Ward has written, but here was a phalanx of crises. As a veteran Washington correspondent had predicted, the emergencies were building up like a coral reef. By late summer Berlin was on the brink, the Southeast Asian dominoes were tottering, and the President, whose back was more painful than the public knew, was both ill and anxious. After his Vienna meeting with Khrushchev his trust in the power of rationalism — a faith which had reached its peak the year before, after his victory in West Virginia, which he believes he won by reasoning — had been replaced by faith in the big battalions. One battalion worked. The President ordered an armed convoy to Berlin, and it traveled the *Autobahn* unmolested. Then Laos was removed, at least for the moment, from the critical list. The Chinese Reds began tarring the Russian Reds, who reciprocated; the drums of the Congo were muffled, and NATO had a stronger look. By November temperatures everywhere were normal. The world, having passed through a minor convulsion, had emerged unchanged.

But the President of the United States had changed. During the first seismic jolts his friends and aides had begun to detect subtle changes in his manner. It was Billings's impression that "Suddenly he was hard to get close to. He was thinking all the time." After a 3 A.M. meeting with the Joint Chiefs over Cuba he walked out through the French windows of his office, through the rose garden, and paced the south grounds alone for half an hour. He had always been a gregarious man. No one could remember his doing anything like that before. Again, when he finished his Berlin speech on July 25, 1961, he turned away from the television cameras, left his office without speaking to anyone, and strode back to the mansion by himself. Jacqueline and the children were on the Cape. Only solitude awaited him, but that was what he needed just then. "He had less time for trivia," says Assistant Secretary of the Navy James A. Reed, another friend from PT days, "and he was more restless." His hand became increasingly active; he was forever pulling up his socks, toying absently with his telephone, arranging papers on his desk and then rearranging them. Fred Holborn, a special presidential assistant, believes that he became more philosophical, and another aide thinks he detected signs of humility. This is not a Kennedy trait — he was a cocky President-Elect — but it is a presidential trait. "There are a great many people, I expect a million in the country, who could have done the job better than I could, but I had the job and I had to do it," Harry Truman said, and while Kennedy didn't go that far, his manner did suggest a tempering.

All his life he had shunned routine. During his senatorial days his aides had been little more than aides-de-camp; he would decide that something needed doing and then, like as not, he would wind up doing it himself. These habits had persisted through his early White House months, when more than one minor figure in the State Department was aghast to find himself dealing directly with the President via telephone. They began to change that summer. In most departments he now deals with the top of the ladder: secretaries and undersecretaries. State has been an exception, but even there he goes no lower than the assistant secretary rung. For the first time he has some sense of the delegation of power and is reasonably comfortable with a staff. The web of system has appeared; briefings of the Chief Executive follow a more orderly pattern. Scheduled conferences have emerged — the Cabinet and the reorganized National Security Council meet twice a month, and each week a Tuesday luncheon group plans security moves, to be followed by a Thursday luncheon group which acts on the plans. He will never be methodical. Every week or so he misplaces his reading spectacles — he's slightly farsighted — and has to acquire new ones, and although he reads rapidly, he's not a good paper mover; the end of each afternoon brings a frantic rescue operation as aides rush in to retrieve memoranda they've left on his desk. He still hates to be told what to do, still dislikes contrived conferences, and still keeps his talks with the Cabinet as brief as possible. But the hectic half-hour appointments of the first year are no more. In middle age his life has finally begun to move in patterns.

The President's work day starts in bed. Each morning a White House butler hands a stack of newspapers to the President's bespectacled Negro valet, who brings them into the bedroom at 7:30 A.M. As James Reston of the New York *Times* noted, Kennedy takes printer's ink for breakfast. While still in his pajamas — or lying in his bathtub, under a board which supports the papers — he examines staff memos, scans every inch of the *Times*, and then riffles through the *Wall Street Journal*, the Baltimore *Sun*, and the Washington *Post*, concentrating on columnists. A line of type may echo around the world. When he read that under Defense policy it was impossible for American soldiers wounded in Vietnam to receive the Purple Heart, he issued an Executive Order reversing the policy. He appears to have total recall; nothing ever seems to be erased from his mind. The results of his morning perusals must be seen to be believed. Once the attitude of American business was being discussed at a Cabinet meeting, and the President, in support of a point, casually cited a quarter-page advertisement which, he said, had been published the previous week in the financial pages of the *Times*. He named the date, the page number, and the ad's position on the page. His ministers were skeptical — none of them had noticed it, not even Secretary of the Treasury Dillon — so the President called for the edition, and there it was, just as he had said. Again, an editorial viewed with alarm his proposal to increase the number of regular Army divisions, and he told Salinger indignantly, "They said just the opposite in another editorial six months ago. Find it." Unlucky Pierre couldn't. He was plowing through a blizzard of newsprint when his phone rang. "I don't know why it takes you so long to put your finger on something," the President complained. "It was in the upper right hand editorial column, and it had some data about battleships." He cited some of the data. Then Pierre discovered it and confirmed him.

By 9 A.M. Kennedy is in his oval office, meeting appointments, after which he takes a fifteen-minute dip in his ninety-degree White House pool. Presidential exertion is sharply limited by Dr. Janet Travell, his physician; since his back injury during an Ottawa tree-planting ceremony in May 1961, his only exercise has been swimming and workouts with dumbbells under the supervision of a Navy chief petty officer, and his freestyle stroke is hampered by a light medical corset which he must wear at all times. After lunch he follows Eisenhower's example and takes a brief siesta. Awakening, he hits his best stride of the day. In the first months he returned to the West Wing and worked there until 7:30, but with the family in Hyannis Port during his first presidential summer, he began spending afternoons in the private apartment. He liked it. Opportunities for reflection were greater; between appointments he could read and think. For a time he was rarely seen in the West Wing after his noon meal. Toward the end of his first year the pendulum began to swing back — with the return of Congress there were more formal meetings — though he still prefers the quiet mansion, and stays there when he can.

At the end of the day bills and correspondence are brought to him for signature. He dines at 8 P.M., while

Sorensen and Mrs. Evelyn Lincoln, the President's personal secretary, assemble his evening reading in a file which is usually delivered by Brigadier General Chester V. Clifton, his military aide. Presidential homework is heavy, and is faithfully done; once an inch-thick report reached him at 10:30 P.M., and the next morning he had finished it and was ready to talk about it. He reads, not in the oval study, but in the west sitting room, which is informal and comfortable and which, since most of its furniture came from the Kennedys' Georgetown house, stirs memories of other days. The only desk is a frail antique. Kennedy doesn't use it. Instead he sprawls on a slip-covered couch, distributing papers on the floor. He writes here, too, scribbling on yellow, ruled, legal-length pads. If the manuscript is a speech, he has help. First drafts are written by Sorensen, and the two men bounce subsequent drafts back and forth, though the speaker naturally has the last word. He uses it, too. He edits phrases up to the moment of delivery and beyond — in the middle of his second State of the Union address he departed from the text, polishing prose from the rostrum.

In the sitting room this writer once watched another guest, a foreign policy adviser, admiring the walls of books. "You know, they put a fine library in my office," he murmured wistfully, "and I haven't had time to turn a page." The President makes time, which, considering his burden of official reading, is something of a feat. Books are saved for weekends, but even then he is accompanied by a heavy black alligator briefcase containing weekly agency reports, background synopses, and — by presidential direction — anything which any ranking member of the Administration feels is important.

This is a sharp change from the Eisenhower chain-of-command concept. As a senator, Kennedy scouted the notion of an administrative Vice President, and as Chief Executive he has abolished Sherman Adams's old job. Ever since a clique of Andrew Jackson's cronies tried to elude public attention by using the White House kitchen door, most Presidents have had a kitchen cabinet — administrative assistants, aides, and advisers who are, in fact, closer to the Chief Executive than full-fledged ministers. Under Eisenhower everyone in both cabinets was assigned a slot in a tidy table of organization. In theory differences anywhere in the government were to be settled down below, by the numbers. In practice a number of feuds worsened; *e.g.*, the Secretary of the Treasury is said to have refused to talk to the Budget Director on the telephone. Senator Kennedy watched this sort of thing with distaste. The State and Defense Departments, he said, were dealing with one another like "so many Venetian envoys." Even if the chain worked perfectly, he was against it; like Winston Churchill he was wary of staffs that can dictate command decisions, and one of his first executive acts was to eliminate Eisenhower's Operations Coordinating

Board and seventeen interdepartmental agencies. His Administration is much more of a one-man show. No one tells him what he will read or whom he will see. Any member of the official family can check with Mrs. Lincoln in the morning and receive a hearing.

The idea is to keep the President posted, to provide him with choices — to give him, as one aide put it, "binocular vision." Seeing the big picture is an old presidential problem. Minutiae keep cluttering up the lenses. "Now go away!" Lincoln told a visitor. "Go away! I cannot attend to all these details. I could as easily bail out the Potomac with a teaspoon!" The Presidency was less than a year old when George Washington confided to a French diplomat that he couldn't even keep up with his correspondence, although, as Sidney Hyman has pointed out, the first President could prepare his budget on a single sheet of paper; one year he appointed only sixty-five officials. A modern budget is a million-and-a-half words long, and Kennedy, who directed a staff of twenty-one men in his senatorial days, is answerable for 2,350,000 employees. Big government is, by its very size, a labyrinth. Henry S. Rowan, a Harvard professor who is serving as Kennedy's Deputy Assistant Secretary of Defense, says the Pentagon alone is like "a log going down the river with twenty-five thousand ants on it, each thinking he's steering." Harry Truman called the whole thing "oppressive." Accurately predicting Eisenhower's difficulties with it, Truman said in 1952, "He'll sit here and he'll say, 'Do this! Do that!' *And nothing will happen.* Poor Ike. It won't be a bit like the Army. He'll find it very frustrating."

A Chief Executive's major problem, said Washington, is "seclusion from information." If it was a crux then, it has since become an enigma, and Kennedy, hoping to profit from the lessons of his predecessors, carefully built competition into his Administration. Each department, for example, has liaison men in it who may report two or three times a day, telling the White House how things are shaping up. Some old-timers in the government look upon these expediters as meddlers, and call them *Kennedystas.* Their resentment is resented by the President. It is his nature to take a hand in all things, and he feels he must stir up Washington's Bumbledom.

School texts still teach that there are three branches to American government: executive, legislative, and judicial. They err. There are four. The executive is split into the President and the bureaucracy, a sprawling, diffuse collection of organisms which has become, in Schlesinger's vivid phrase, "this exasperating Jello." By far the most gelatinous department is State. The President's failure to turn over State's goo depresses him, as it depressed his predecessors, and his determination to do something about it led to a shakeup of Foggy Bottom ten months after his inaugural. The appointment of George W. Ball as undersecretary has given him some sense of anchorage there. He is sanguine about his ambassadors and McNamara's strong role in Defense, and he has no sense of sabotage in the Treasury. State, Defense, and the Treasury — the big three — are familiar to the President now. The same cannot be said for lesser departments. Because of his concentration on foreign affairs and the economy he has had to watch some domestic issues out of the corner of his eye. Secretary of the Interior Stewart L. Udall's attempts to catch his full attention have left Udall frustrated, and despite Secretary of Agriculture Orville Freeman's new program, most of the President's knowledge of farms seems to have been acquired in the Wisconsin primary of 1960. At this writing he finds Agriculture and Interior rather mysterious, meaning that data about them goes into the evening file, into the weekend briefcase.

"I *need* information," he says, "and I get a lot." It comes to him diversely — from an eighteen-button telephone console in his office, from radiophones in presidential cars and planes, from a Signal Corps contraption a few feet from his desk which can tape sounds on almost any wave length in the world and rebroadcast them at his convenience, and via powerful new generators which have been installed on the Kennedy yacht *Marlin* to relay coded messages when he is aboard. Much of the material he receives is solicited. Newspaper editors invited to lunch with the President are asked to bring memos on problems in their areas. When he asks private citizens to send him

proposals, as he did in the Berlin speech, he is in
dead earnest. "Roosevelt got most of his ideas from
talking to people," he told Professor James M. Burns
of Williams College. "I get most of mine from reading." But he gets many ideas from people, too. Indeed, he is extremely effective during meetings *à deux*.
In Washington — "the City of Conversation," Henry
James called it — Kennedy has become the conver-
sationalist-in-chief. On a platform he lacks Churchill's
pulpit touch; he is at his best in dialogue. Gore Vidal,
a friend of the Kennedys, remarks that "Those who
like him tend to tell him everything. You feel he ought
to know, and he's terrifically interested. He's really a
great gossip." Mention an acquaintance, an ally, or a
potential antagonist in 1964, and John Kennedy is instantly alert. Have you seen him lately? he wants to
know. How is he? What's he doing? Is such-and-such
true? His curiosity ranges beyond official Washington
— when *Advise and Consent* was being filmed, he
phoned the set one night for a progress report —
though it is felt most keenly, of course, in the government. "This morning he called me at eight-fifteen and
asked me for advice," Larry O'Brien, his master politician, said during a day of intricate congressional
maneuvering. "That doesn't mean he'll follow it. Later
I found he was calling a lot of other people, too."
Dean Rusk and Douglas Dillon are summoned to the
West Wing two or three times a week for interroga-
tions, and Edward R. Murrow, director of the United

States Information Agency, calls his White House telephone "the blowtorch."

The President has been called the best reporter in Washington. In 1945, as a correspondent, he covered the birth of the U.N. and wrote analyses of European politics. Arthur Krock recalls that although Kennedy was merely a green cub, he was virtually the only unbiased writer to predict Churchill's defeat in Britain's general election that year. Merriman Smith, the senior White House correspondent, believes that his news skill is one reason that few biting questions are asked of him now in press conferences. The questioners are wary, Smith reasons, because "a reporter who tackles him poorly prepared is liable to be shown up before a nation-wide audience." Certainly Kennedy has the journalist's gift for seizing conversational initiative; a visiting writer is very likely to emerge from the Executive Mansion with the disquieting realization that the President has been interviewing *him*.

"What do they want me to do?" he says of his critics. "Why don't they put it down on paper?" One criticism which has been put down is that he is getting too *much* information, that he has veered from the red tape of the Eisenhower staff system to the opposite extreme. The President "did not want a Cabinet of the traditional kind," according to his old government teacher at Harvard, emeritus Professor Arthur N. Holcombe. "What he wanted was energetic and

efficient department management." But the objectors
insist that true efficiency can only be found in even
more frequent Cabinet meetings, and more important, in the correct use of channels. Too many presidential task forces are swimming around Washington,
the argument runs; the White House staff has become an undisciplined herd. The new Administration
has "done a good job of confusing me and all my
friends," Eisenhower complained, during a speech in
which he went on to predict an inflation that would
curl your hair.

Of course, what confuses Gettysburg needn't baffle
the rest of the country — Eisenhower was sometimes
bewildered by the Administration that preceded
Kennedy's — and whether the government should be
run like the Army or a PT squadron is an open-end
question anyhow. Every President has his own system; Lincoln (as William H. Seward scornfully
noted) kept his files in the sweatband of his stovepipe
hat. Actually Kennedy's part of the operation, the
bridge of the flagship, is neat as a bandbox. As a
World War II naval officer the CO once received a
low rating in military bearing and neatness; and when
he took off for his most memorable sea action, the PT
base lacked a record of the men aboard because he
had neglected to see to it that a muster sheet was
turned in to headquarters. That couldn't happen now.
In his forties he is all spit and polish, and he expects
his subordinates to be competent executives. The
public sawing-in-half of Chester Bowles during the

New Frontier's first year had nothing to do with Bowles's ideas. Someone had told the President that Bowles was a good administrator, and someone had been dead wrong. Adlai Stevenson, on the other hand, has won presidential admiration because he turned the United States U.N. operation, which was jerry, into America's best-run embassy. Kennedy and Stevenson will never be a perfect fit, but their relationship is far better than anyone had expected it to be. There is candor between them, and respect, and the President is impressed by Stevenson's intellectual depth and sinew.

"If a democracy cannot produce able leaders its chance for survival is slight," John Kennedy wrote during his last year with Professor Holcombe. A Roosevelt or a Lincoln wouldn't correlate leadership with managerial ability. A Kennedy does, and he has developed remarkable gifts for personal command. He knows precisely when to lose his temper with an underling — flushing and sharpening his New England vowels — and when to recover it so the scar will heal quickly. His assumption of responsibility is total. There have been no private recriminations over bad advice, not even after Cuba; indeed, his restraint then served to weld the new Administration together. He's not blindly loyal. He just waits. Bowles was carted off eventually, and Allen Dulles became a retired spy — after the heat was off. When one of his men is in the soup, he tries to extricate him; G. Mennen Williams inflamed Europe by announcing that Africa should be for the Africans, and the President wondered aloud who else Africa should be for. It was no answer, but it did shift the spotlight away from Soapy's embarrassment.

Perhaps Kennedy's most effective administrative tool is his memory. "He can still drive down an avenue in Boston," one of his political lieutenants has said, "and remember which stores put up his campaign posters ten years ago." There is some sleight of hand here. No one could recall as much as he seems to. He has a way of recollecting a fragment of an incident — the circumstances under which he met someone, say — and revealing this in such a way that the man leaves with the impression that his name, rank, and serial number are indelibly fixed in the President's mind. Yet even when the most skeptical reservations are made, examples of his retention are astonishing. During the Los Angeles convention he needed no notes; he knew every delegate's preference, down to the half-vote. The whole country watched his extemporaneous performance in the campaign debates, and since then he has displayed familiarity with Geneva conferences which were reported in the *Times* when he was at Choate. After a 1962 press conference Reston wrote: "How he knew the precise drop in milk consumption in 1960, the percentage rise in textile imports from 1957 to 1960, and the number of speeches cleared by the Defense Department last year — 1,200 — is not quite clear, but anyway, he did."

One evening the President was discussing a judicial appointment with four friends, among them James A. Reed and a writer. "I'm not so sure lawyers are as infallible as you think," Kennedy said to the writer. "I remember some trouble Jim here had in a firm." He then proceeded to retell a story Reed had told him ten years before. "*I* had forgotten all about it," Jim said afterward. "Suddenly I realized that he was practically quoting me verbatim — that his account was almost word-for-word the one I'd given him then. It was uncanny." These tape recorder performances are so extraordinary that people who don't know the President often refuse to credit them. Shortly after his second State of the Union speech Kennedy received a brief visit from Floyd Patterson. Feeling the heavyweight champion's muscles, the President chatted with him about past Patterson bouts, episodes in the fighter's career, and possible challengers. Bystanders assumed he had been briefed. "He not only hadn't been briefed," Salinger said afterward. "I didn't even know he followed the fights."

Genius for detail is not genius. It won't raze Berlin's wall or reduce Castro, and were it compulsive it could become a big waste of what is, after all, the most valuable time in the nation. Kept in check, though, it is a handy device. The boss may not remember everything, but if his staff thinks he does, the effect is the same. Kennedy is careful to cultivate that impression. He has a disturbing way of giving orders so casually ("Do this for me, will you?") that newcomers aren't sure he's serious. Six weeks later, in the middle of another discussion, he will turn to the man responsible and inquire — as though opening a book at a bookmark — "Did you make that call?" In consequence the White House has learned that *no* task may be treated lightly. He has been known to take an interest in individual expense accounts, and even typists have been disciplined. Signing nearly half a ream of routine letters daily, he can still pick out errors. Passing one girl's desk he inquired, "What was the idea of waiting a month to answer a letter?" A typical display of Kennedy mnemonics followed: a recitation of the date of the original letter, the name of the correspondent, the date of the reply. "To spot that one," the girl's supervisor points out, "he had to read the answer *and* the original underneath. And that was one of a batch of two hundred that day."

Compared to the incoming mail that day, Kennedy's two hundred replies were only a mite. Stenographers may believe that an omniscient President is meeting all the demands on his office. The White House postman knows better, and the weight of his bag gives some inkling of the gap between what is asked of a Chief Executive and what can be done. Each week Kennedy himself receives some seventeen thousand letters — even Caroline gets four hundred — offering blessings, giving advice, making requests. Many follow familiar patterns. The bag usually contains some mimeographed stuff, inspired by lobbies. Since this represents no individual effort, it gets no individual attention. It is simply dumped. During the school year a thousand letters arrive weekly from classrooms. These are handled more gently. Another thousand ask for pictures of the President (they get them) and copies of his autograph (they get facsimiles). Other correspondents believe it is more blessed to give. Among the letters there are always some bundles and crates. The custom of sending presents to the potentate goes back to the days of myrrh, and democracy hasn't altered it. Thomas Jefferson received a 1235-pound cheese from a Massachusetts town. John Quincy Adams acquired floral specimens; Andrew Jackson, clay pipes; Franklin Roosevelt, stamps. Lemonade Lucy Hayes got a lot of lemons. John Kennedy's packages contain handicrafts, curios, and Indian headdresses, which are turned over to the National Archives; rocking chairs, rugs, clothing, and jewelry, which are returned with thanks; and books, which are kept.

When all the routine mail has been set aside, however, the balance of correspondence is still heavily in the public's favor, and the best Kennedy can do is make sure that his evening file includes samples from the lot, with every fiftieth or hundredth epistle — depending on the pressure of other business — marked for his attention. Some of them make curious reading. People complain about inflation, taxes, social security, unemployment, *apartheid*, Krishna Menon, television commercials. A Pennsylvania woman wondered why he said "I shall" instead of "I will." She knew her grammar, but felt there wasn't sufficient determination in the expression of "mere futurity." A Marine's wife denounced "that Hiss brainchild, the United Nations charter." A Minneapolis constituent wanted him to investigate foreign aid, start testing bombs, quit talking about disarmament, listen more attentively to the Senate Internal Security Subcommittee, do something about Outer Mongolia, invade Cuba — and cut the budget.

Individual missives are absurd, but in sum they are touching. They represent an instinctive turning to leadership which transcends the sophistications of American politics. In Washington it is hard to see this. The capital thinks in terms of Administrations, but out where the postmarks are affixed these distinctions become blurred. There Americans have a tendency to lump Presidents together — since the 1960 inaugural the White House has received mail addressed to every occupant from Coolidge to Eisenhower. To most of his constituents John Kennedy is one of a line of men, and because he stands where Jefferson and Lincoln stood, their light falls on his shoulders. The typical American, Clinton Rossiter wrote, thinks of his Chief Executive "as a combination scoutmaster, Delphic oracle, hero of the silver screen, and father of the multitudes." He is, said Sidney Hyman, "the guide and interpreter of public opinion, the keeper of the conscience, the ceremonial head, the disciplinarian and the source of clemency," and Theodore H. White called him "the nation's chief educator, the nation's chief persuader." As every taxpayer knows, he is also the chief public servant. The house at 1600 Pennsylvania Avenue is the public's property, and in time of stress its owners eye it anxiously. It is always watched these days. On the sidewalks the silent men press against the fence, peering up. From above the view is startling — it dismayed Jacqueline Kennedy at first — but the watchers mean well. Their stares, like the letters and the bundled tributes, are mute offerings. The people want to do something. They want to give their President direct, immediate help.

And they can't. "So many of the banalities are correct," a member of Kennedy's kitchen cabinet says. "It *is* the loneliest job in the world." Part of "the extraordinary isolation imposed upon the President," as Woodrow Wilson called it, is inherent in the system. Congressmen work with other congressmen; Supreme Court justices with other justices; but there are only two superpower chieftains in the world, and to talk shop the President must go to the summit, which has proved to be not only profitless but disagreeable. If he is to fill his office properly he cannot even lean on men of his own party. To meet vital issues he must be prepared to break away from party and appeal to the entire nation. Lincoln felt the strain of this solitude when he moved to make the Emancipation Proclamation; so did Wilson when, for ten days in 1917, he wrestled with his war message.

But Wilson could share that decision. In those days Congress still declared war. No more; since the Formosa Resolution making war is a presidential matter. The atom has given the Chief Executive what Dean Rusk describes as an "almost unbearable responsibility." It is a cruel fact of our time that the graver the choice, the fewer the men who may make it. Nuclear tests were resumed by decree; no other way was open. In most matters of foreign policy John Kennedy confers with Rusk, McNamara, the Attorney General, Mac Bundy, Lyndon Johnson, John McCone, General Maxwell Taylor, and the Joint Chiefs, but if he must act quickly, he may consult only the first three, and should the big question arise — the need for a retaliatory attack after absorbing an enemy blow — he would have only his own counsel. He alone can launch a Minuteman capable of destroying a fourth of Moscow after a twenty-minute run. Among the obligations which he must never forget, this is the first, and among the reasons why he cannot forget is that visible evidence of it is never far from him. The code which would launch total thermonuclear attack is kept in a slender black case bearing a double lock. This case is constantly in possession of one of a team of five Army warrant officers. The warrant officer on duty goes wherever the President goes. They spell each other, but no one can spell John Kennedy. In Hyannis Port, Palm Beach, or Middleburg, Virginia, that burden follows the President of the United States. It is the most harrowing game of solitaire in

:he world, and there is only that other player, co-
existing on the other side of the globe.

The President glides through the lovely apartment,
moving slowly, escorting his guest to the elevator.
Two floors below, a crew-cut Secret Service man
awaits the descent; near him an inconspicuously
dressed warrant officer keeps the vigil; but here there
is only a host and his guest, chatting about mutual acquaintances. The suite is still as still. Flowered drapes
have been drawn across the broad west window,
masking the rose garden; eastward, moonbeams
freckle the old green roof of the Treasury; within, tiny
points of light twinkle on a hall spinet, on a picture of
Princess Stanislas Radziwill, on a framed snapshot of
young Jacqueline Bouvier with her father and on another of Caroline romping with hers. The President's
hand reaches for the elevator button and is withdrawn. He wants to say something else. He says it,
and the hand rises and falls again. And again. And
then again.

The conversation is idle. The guest, a person of no
consequence, senses that he is merely someone who
will listen, that this is the end of the day, and that
when he leaves there will be no one. He wants to help,
and he can't, and abruptly he understands all the
earnest letter-writers and donors of useless gifts and
simple starers — all those who reach so far and still
cannot touch, because none can reach here.

Now everything has been said. The fisting hand

opens and brushes the button. The black wrough
steel door slides open.

"Just press G — ground floor," says the flat Ne
England voice. "Goodnight." And John Kenned
walks back toward the oval study by himself: alon

TWO

The Establishmentarian

Two DAYS after his U.N. disarmament speech in the fall of 1961 the President of the United States boarded his ninety-two-foot cabin cruiser for a twenty-minute run on Narragansett Bay. It was a gaudy autumn day. *Honey Fitz* wore a bustle of sparkling foam. The man who had cruised these waters as a World War II lieutenant (j.g.) was in a blithe mood, and as he passed Newport Naval Station sailors greeted his little flagship with a twenty-one-gun salute.

"This isn't so bad, Mr. President," an appreciative guest observed.

John Kennedy grinned. "It's a lot better than having your ears beaten in by Goodie Knight in California," he said.

Richard Nixon, beached on the West Coast, would have winced at that. That week he was pinned down by the political artillery of Goodwin Knight, then his chief Republican gubernatorial rival, and the President's remark underscored the fact that Nixon's plight was a direct consequence of his loss to Kennedy the previous fall. In 1960 the two men whose lives are now so far apart were separated by some 120,000 votes, less than one-fifth of one per cent of the popular vote. The winner had won a photo-finish — "a miracle," he himself called it. He had just managed to resolder the old Roosevelt coalition of labor, northern minority groups, and the South, and it had taken some doing, not all of which had been visible on the television debates. He attracted a big Negro vote by expressing sympathy for Martin Luther King, but he also found it expedient to confer with a Southern governor and the head of the state's White Citizens' Council, who endorsed him the moment the conference was over. A writer inquired of this peculiar coincidence, "How did that happen?" Kennedy shrugged and replied, "Just lucky, I guess."

There was that, too. There has always been that. His father once called him a "lucky mush," and others have noted chance's uncanny habit of backstopping him. By some strange process he even wins when he loses. Shortly after the Cuban caper his Gallup rating reached a new high, and he himself remarked wryly,

"It seems as though the more mistakes I make, the more popular I become." Big Steel's rhubarb was called "a domestic Cuba" by one pundit, but three days later Steel collapsed, and there stood Jack the giant-killer — "almost making you believe," Lem Billings said at the time, "that he has the touch of the supernatural on his shoulder." The steel Donnybrook reminded Billings of 1956. Chosen that summer to put Adlai Stevenson's name in nomination, Senator Kennedy found that he had a chance for second place on the Democrat ticket, and he went for it. In far-off France there was a muffled explosion. Joe Kennedy, vacationing there, felt that he was making a hideous mistake. "I was sure Adlai would lose," the ambassador recalled shortly after the Narragansett Bay outing, "and that his defeat would be blamed on Jack's Catholicism." Jack came within an eyelash of becoming the vice-presidential choice; his defeat was variously blamed on his backing of the Benson farm policy, the dismantling of the convention's totalizer score board, and some peculiar behavior by Delegate John W. McCormack of Massachusetts. Yet none of these offered much consolation. The blunt truth was that he had been beaten. Next day the New York *Herald Tribune* commented, "The famous Kennedy luck ran out today." It hadn't, though. Things were just the other way round. Stevenson went down anyhow, but the sacrificial lamb was Estes Kefauver, while the nation remembered young Kennedy smiling cheerfully at his Chicago rebuff. He himself was among the first to grasp the significance of this. Told that he would be a cinch for the number two spot after Eisenhower's second term, he replied, "I'm not running for the Vice Presidency any more. I'm running for the Presidency." During the next four years he barnstormed the country, and sure enough, by the summer of 1960 he had become his party's front runner.

Before his nomination he was relaxing on the Cypress Point, California, golf course with Red Fay. On the 150-yard fifteenth hole, Fay recalls, the candidate-to-be teed off with a seven iron and almost got a hole-in-one. As the ball rolled across the green Kennedy leaped up and down, shouting at it, "Get out of there!" "What's the matter?" Fay cried. "You crazy?" Kennedy wasn't crazy. He was just thinking ahead. "If it drops in," he explained rapidly, "everybody in the country will know about it in five minutes, and they'll think another golfer is trying to get into the White House. Get *out* of there!" The ball then stopped, inches from the cup.

His luck has held so often that long ago it generated an enviable optimism. Even in the buggy, virescent trough of the Solomons his favorite song was "Blue Skies." Somehow, despite his vitality and his nervous mannerisms, he conveys an impression of quiet confidence. "If it were not so calm, if it were more strident and pushful, it would be plain arrogance," Stewart Alsop once commented. Occasionally it has come close to arrogance. Proposing to Jacqueline Bouvier, he informed her that he had actually decided to marry her a year before. He hadn't been ready then; now he was. "How *big* of you!" she cried. But while this suggests that he was sure of himself, he wasn't too sure, since after all, she did accept him. Things have had a way of working out that way — his way. Asked before his presidential campaign how he proposed to win the election, he replied easily, "In the debates." After he had done precisely that, he chose Ben Smith, a former Harvard roommate, to fill out his Senate term, and Mrs. Smith, riffling through an old diary of her husband's, found this 1941 note: *Saw Jack again today and we settled the affairs of the world.* Jack himself had first won the title of senator by challenging Henry Cabot Lodge, the incumbent, in 1952. That was the year of the first Eisenhower avalanche. Late in election night the challenger took a walk in the Boston Public Garden with another ex-roommate, Torbert Macdonald. Eisenhower was sweeping the state, Lodge was in the lead. But John Kennedy not only assumed victory; he had gone beyond it. To Macdonald he said thoughtfully, "I wonder what job Eisenhower's going to give Lodge?" Six hours later Lodge conceded, and a blizzard of good wishes descended upon the new champ. He always seems to get more than his share of good wishes — his presidential mail is twice as large as Eisenhower's — perhaps because he has a curious way of involving people, including opponents, in his struggles. After a trying convalescence in 1955 he found a huge basket of fruit in his senatorial office. The card read, *Welcome home — Dick Nixon.*

This is the stuff of legend: the luck of the Irish, Roscommon arisen. Boston Irishmen love legends. In Somerville and Charlestown many a man regarded the verdict of 1960 as the final vindication of the Ould Sod. Strolling around the Massachusetts State House with the President's younger brother Ted, this writer encountered an elderly Curley satellite. "Well, the Yankees are finally whipped!" trumpeted the man, whose first name is actually Patsy. The writer ventured that Beacon Hill's power had been broken at least a generation ago, but Patsy rambled on with the wild inconsistency of an Edwin O'Connor character. "Now," he said darkly, "we got to watch out for the Guineas. Ever notice how a Guinea cries in jail? No spirit, no spirit at all. I'd rather work with a Jew than a Guinea. The only people that are happy in jail are the niggers. Niggers have a grand time in the can, because they can sleep all the time," Patsy reflected. "But the worst of the lot are the Yankees. They're *prejudiced.*"

Clearly there is something bogus here. Boston's ethnic loyalties are a carryover from the days when, as John Kennedy has observed, each wave of immigrants "disliked and distrusted the next." The Irish, probably because they spoke English, became the leaders of the downtrodden. But the notion that they have always been a deprived proletarian race doesn't hold up. From Ireland came the Duke of Wellington, Lord Kitchener, and Montgomery of Alamein; even St. Patrick's name was Patricius Magnus, which indicates that he was gently born. American Paddies have also done rather well, and not only recently. Among the Presidents of Irish descent are Andrew Jackson and Chester A. Arthur. Well before the potato famine, which ended some time ago, there were Irish aristocrats in this country, and while it's not generally known in Somerville, the White House itself was designed by a native of Ireland. Its classic façade was inspired by a house in Dublin.

Of course, bigotry was a nuisance. Yet Boston's Hibernians have given as good as they got. If it was impossible for a pre-Kennedy Catholic to be President, it was, and continues to be, almost impossible for anyone else to hold local office. And it is notable that southern Europeans, although fully qualified members of the Church, are excluded from the religious martyrdom. As Kenneth Galbraith commented sardonically in a review of an O'Connor novel, there is a feeling "that the Irish soul is an exceptionally sensitive and friable organ that provides unlimited opportunities for study." Larry O'Brien may confess that "these days it's hard to tell the difference between the Irish and the Yankee Irish," but to the O'Briens of an older generation this is cultural miscegenation. For them the President is a magnificent symbol. In their minds his presence at 1600 Pennsylvania Avenue represents absolution from outrageous fortune and three-decker tenements. Pat and Mike have finally put the Cabots and Lowells in their places — or rather, Himself has done it, which is the same thing, since he is one of them.

It's a grand myth, and if you reach far enough into the past you can find a cast. Himself is a descendant of one Pat Kennedy, who left an Erin hamlet with the fine emerald name of New Ross, Wexford County, a century ago and landed on East Boston's Noodle Island during that eight-year period when the British lack of interest in parity was driving over a million Irishmen to the United States. Pat's son Patrick J., for whom another presidential cabin cruiser is now named, grew black handle-bar mustaches, ran a saloon, and became a local Democratic leader, at various times holding office as fire commissioner, street commissioner, election commissioner, and state representative; and Patrick J.'s son Joseph P. Kennedy married the daughter of a pol celebrated for his public renditions of "Sweet Adeline."

This gifted tenor was John F. "Honey Fitz" Fitzgerald, or *"El Dulce Adelino,"* as he was hailed by Franklin Roosevelt, who never missed an ethnic bet. With Honey Fitz the tale grows richer. He had been brought up in an authentic eight-family tenement not far from the old North Church. In his teens he had been a clerk under Leverett Saltonstall, grandfather of the present senator. He went on to become Boston's first mayor of Irish parentage, only to have his own senatorial ambitions foiled in 1916 by another eminent modern Republican's grandfather, Henry Cabot Lodge, Sr., the bugbear of Woodrow Wilson and a silkstocking who is remembered for his fight to stifle immigration. Add the fact that Honey's own five-year-old grandson, Jack Kennedy, tagged along on one of his campaigns and functioned as an audience of one while the old man rehearsed his speeches, and the fable seems complete.* It is more leprechaunish than *The Last Hurrah,* if less plausible.

The trouble with it is that it omits a key character — Jack's father — and the ambassador is not the sort of man you ignore. Irish-Americans are supposed to be fun-loving but indigent. As a boy of eight Joe Kennedy had revealed an entrepreneural mutation, peddling candy and peanuts on Boston excursion boats, and he had gone on to shatter the cultural pattern by graduating from Harvard ('12). In college he had been a poor economics student, which is like pointing out that Einstein flunked math, because when Joe entered banking he became a wizard of such tricky stock dodges as market rigging, matched orders, margin manipulation, and washed and short sales. In one of President Kennedy's favorite suspense novels a character remarks that "to become very rich you have to be helped by a combination of remarkable circum-

* An illusion. At this writing Ted Kennedy has taken dead aim on the United States Senate. The Republican marksman is George Cabot Lodge, thirty-four, the son of the President's 1952 victim and the grandson of Honey's 1916 nemesis. In senatorial years Boston may become the city where the Lodges speak only to denounce the Kennedys, and vice versa.

stances and an unbroken run of luck. . . . At the beginning, getting together the first ten thousand, or the first hundred thousand, things have to go damn right." Things never went wrong for Joe. He never gave them a chance. By the skillful use of sheer money he multiplied his fortune again and again, amassing the astounding sum of two hundred and fifty million dollars.

Wealth can't change a man's background. During a political strategy conference a few years ago, one of Jack's advisers hinted that the ambassador wouldn't appreciate the average man's point of view. "What do you mean?" Joe flared. "I happen to be the most average guy in this whole damned outfit." Like many tycoons he has sometimes tended to exaggerate his humble origins — as Abe Martin observed, the older a man gets, the farther he had to walk to school as a boy — yet he had a point. His earthy, on-the-make manner has reached men baffled by the sophistication of his son's Administration. Though a financier, Joe was a maverick during his money-making years. According to Arthur Krock, he didn't acquire status until Franklin Roosevelt, anxious to stamp out the practices which had made men like him rich, appointed him to the Securities and Exchange Commission. Roosevelt decided that only an insider could do the job and asked Krock to write a flattering story about Joe, paving the way for his confirmation. The appointee served 431 days as chairman and became respectable, but under his veneer he was still the im-

proper Bostonian. Once two of his new associates protested his habit of playing classical records after every
session. "You dumb bastards don't appreciate culture," he replied.

Money can, however, provide a new background
for the next generation. Joe's did. With his first roll he
left Boston for the suburb of Brookline, and he has
kept going ever since. His children don't share his
heritage. Their mother didn't hang out wash in the
back yard. They were raised in villas, with the merry
chatter of ticker tape on the front porch in the summer, and their shirts have not only white collars, but
monograms. They don't fit the legend at all. The
President isn't parochial; he doesn't speak with a
brogue; he never dances a jig or sings "Danny Boy."
In fact, there is little sentiment in him. "I once asked
him if he'd ever fallen desperately, hopelessly in love,"
James M. Burns recalls, "and he just shrugged and
said, 'I'm not the heavy lover type.'" He's not the pal
type, either. After the inaugural one of his oldest and
most devoted Boston supporters let it be known that
he was interested in a federal judgeship. It would
have been a safe appointment — Massachusetts is,
after all, John Kennedy's political fief. The aspirant
was close to the ambassador, and after Joe's stroke the
nomination would have been accepted as a tender
gesture. Honey Fitz would have rushed it through.
Honey's grandson didn't. "The President seems determined to get as far as possible from the Al Smith
stereotype," Burns says, and a member of the White

House staff suggests that "Kennedy's appreciation of Ireland is merely a literary appreciation." The green label just won't stick to him. When Robert Frost advised him to "be more Irish than Harvard," he could scarcely respond. The President knew Robert Frost, he knew Harvard. But Irish? He hasn't a single mannerism of the shanty Irish, the lace-curtain Irish, or even what Jim Curley leeringly called "the cut-glass Irish." Try to imagine him in a cocked derby and all visions of shamrocks vanish.

Paul Dever, former Governor of Massachusetts, once remarked that "Jack is the first Irish Brahmin." If by Brahmin he meant Yankee blueblood, even this is doubtful. The President's ties with New England are surprisingly slight. He used his state as a springboard to national leadership and then decimated the local party. About all he has in common with Boston now are his affection for the Red Sox, some paintings his wife borrowed from the Boston Museum of Fine Arts, and his accent, which is chiefly evocative of Harvard Yard (although Joe Kennedy calls McCarthy "McCardy," his son sounds the dental). Jack was born in the Brookline house, which was recently repainted light gray by public-spirited volunteers, but he remembers little of those years. His father, a titan at thirty, was acquiring homes in Palm Beach and Bronxville, New York, to which he moved his growing family when the future President was nine years old. Jack didn't live in the Hub again until he prepared to run for Congress after World War II. At that time virtually the only constituent he knew was his aging grandfather. To establish a legal residence he rented a living room and bedroom suite at the hotel where Honey was living, the Bellevue, directly across the street from the Massachusetts State House. Later he moved a few doors away, to 122 Bowdoin Street, apartment 36. His mother installed wall-to-wall carpeting — it is still there — and when he voted for himself in 1960, that was the address he signed to the register. Yet he has rarely been there. Apartment 36 has served a number of valuable functions. For a time it was a way station for legislators from outlying districts. Once Jacqueline went there to be interviewed, with her husband, on Murrow's *Person-to-Person* program. And in the second year of the New Frontier its rather shabby furniture was being used by supporters of Ted Kennedy's Senate candidacy. At no time, however, has it been a genuine home, and long before Richard Nixon offended California Democrats by referring to the President as a "carpetbagger" some disgruntled Bostonians were calling their most famous citizen just that.

William V. Shannon of the New York *Post* compared John Kennedy to an Oxonian who leaves London to stand for Commons in a provincial town where he is known but his family isn't. Charles Spalding, a Kennedy friend, has likened the family to English Whigs of a century ago, and another observer believes that the ambassador resembles the old school British nob who expects his sons to excel in various professions. To the professional Irishman all these parallels are odious, but they are valid. The very rich are, after all, the aristocracy of capitalism. The size of Joe's bank account had made his name familiar in a number of households both in and out of Boston — as an undergraduate Jack saw his family lampooned by Sophie Tucker and Victor Moore in *Leave It to Me* — and before the war his eldest son was being groomed for public office.

In photographs Joseph P. Kennedy, Jr., is his father to the life. They were similar in other ways: hearty, brilliant, outgoing. In 1940 young Joe was elected as a delegate (anti-Roosevelt) to the Democratic National Convention. He was about to set course for Washington, and no one who ever met him doubted he would make it. Then the war intervened. The hope of the clan went down heroically on a volunteer attempt to bomb the Nazis' key V-2 base, leaving Jack as the oldest surviving son. A few weeks after Japan's surrender Jim Curley hurrahed his way back into the mayoralty of Boston, and a former naval person found himself on the streets of the Eleventh Massachusetts Congressional District, running for Curley's empty seat. The candidate was gaunt and awkward. "He was meant to be a writer and a thinker," says Krock. "He made himself over. When Joe died I thought the political genius of the family was gone, but this one has just as much charm as his brother." In 1946, however, Jack lacked his brother's confidence. Before the war he had tried for his Harvard class presidency and failed. Now he painfully wrote out his fifteen-minute speeches in longhand and memorized them verbatim. The business manager of that campaign still has some of the manuscripts. "If Joe were alive I wouldn't be in this," Jack told the voters diffidently. "I'm only trying to fill his shoes."

He filled them — and Honey climbed on a table and sang *"El Dulce Adelino"* — after a madcap primary battle in which he outbarnstormed nine other candidates, including an ex-WAC major who wore her uniform and two Italians who were both named Joseph Russo. Along the way he acquired political style and revealed the first flashes of the wit which is now famous. (At one picnic each of his opponents was introduced as a Bostonian who had come up "the hard way." For obvious reasons, that was dropped from Jack's introduction, so he began by explaining, "I'm the one who didn't come up the hard way.") His spectacular career since then tends to obscure the fact that if Joe were alive, he probably wouldn't be in this. Still, it remains a fact, and a tantalizing one. Where would he be if his brother had lived?

So adroit a politician has he become that some of his acquaintances insist he would be precisely where he is. "Politics was in his blood, waiting to come out," says O'Brien. "He'd have found his way to it," Lem Billings says. Because the war changed everything, there is no way of telling. Certainly he showed no political bent before then. At Harvard he did major in government, but he was chiefly interested in foreign affairs — when he did write a paper on domestic politics, he chose to study an unknown Republican. In the brief hiatus between his graduation and wartime service, he vacillated. He thought of Yale Law School, decided he preferred Stanford Business School, changed his mind after six months there and took off for a trip through South America. Jim Reed believes he would have become an attorney, if only for a time. The President himself is among those who wonder what would have become of him, and he says today, "I'm sure I would have gone to law school after the war. Beyond that, I can't say. I was at loose ends. I was interested in ideas, and I might have gone into journalism. The exchange of ideas that goes with teaching attracted me, but" — he shakes his head — "scholarship requires a special kind of discipline; it wouldn't be my strength."

Yet once he felt otherwise about faculty life. Six years after he succeeded Curley he was campaigning for the Senate in Amherst, the site of the University of Massachusetts and small, heavily endowed Amherst College. His appearance in the university's Old Chapel was a great success. Student questions were good; he was in top form, and afterward he felt exhilarated. Leaving town, his car passed through the handsome Amherst College campus. He turned to O'Brien, commented on the class differences between the two schools, and nodded in the direction of the less ivied state institution. "If it hadn't been for the death of my brother," he said, "I'd probably be teaching in some place like that."

His preference for the red-brick university was revealing. It was an expression of the helping hand ideal, which in turn arises from the political faith of a small, influential elite: the patricians of the Democratic party. The creed of this elite seems to be far closer to the core of John Kennedy than Erin, the Hub, or the Pope. Its roots may be traced to Thomas Jefferson, and it has played a vital, if controversial, role in our national life. Sidney Hyman wrote admiringly that "if there is any recurrent political pattern" in the Presidency, "it is that the troubled conscience of men who inherit wealth often makes them far more generous and resilient in their social attitudes than the self-made man with his purse-proud 'good conscience.'" George Humphrey, contrarily, made the caustic observation that Democrats were led by men who succeeded to their fortunes and Republicans by those who had made their own, and any American of the veteran generation can remember how bitterly Franklin Roosevelt was denounced as a traitor to his class.

Theodore Roosevelt was similarly regarded; so, in many quarters, is the present Governor of New York, for the tradition still has an enclave in the G.O.P. Nevertheless, rich Democrats are the most enthusiastic sharers of the wealth, and in or out of office Kennedy would have been one of them. Reared with what used to be called the advantages, he is, as Lippmann has said, a "thoroughbred." And there was never a chance that he might turn Republican. His father, for one, would have been shocked. People recall the ambassador's isolationism and call him a reactionary; they overlook his stanch support of New Deal legislation. In the crucial year of 1936 he published a book, *I'm For Roosevelt,* sharply rebuking fellow financiers who opposed F.D.R. Until his recent stroke he was decrying Republican dominance over the American press, and his scathing language — scathing even for him — was especially striking because some of his targets were among his oldest personal friends. His continuing loyalty to his party may be puzzling, but it is as real as his millions, and John Kennedy, receiving massive transfusions of both, was fated to follow that line of *noblesse oblige* whose leaders, until his inaugural, were Adlai Stevenson, Averell Harriman, and Thomas Finletter.

Like any caste, this one has its quirks, tabus, and high signs. Some are complex, even inexplicable. No member in good standing, for example, would dream of surrendering dignity to political expedience. In 1960 Kennedy gave the voters restrained Harvard prose (he felt his opponent talked down to the people), and it was some time before he could bring himself to allude publicly to his wife's election-year pregnancy, despite its appeal. Nor do individuals in the patriciate see any conflict between their sympathy for other ranks and their own elegant tastes. The President smokes H. Uppman's cigars — long, thin, and expensive, the brand of Edward VII — and he patronizes Harriman's and Finletter's New York tailor, H. Harris & Co., whose other clients include Nelson Aldrich Rockefeller.

Because so many men of means are Republicans, there is a great deal of interfaith mingling. After Jacqueline Kennedy had appointed a fine arts advisory committee for the White House it turned out that three out of four members were members of the other party. The President's Palm Beach neighbors are overwhelmingly Republican, and so are the citizens of Hyannis Port, who gave over sixty per cent of their vote to Richard Nixon in 1960, just as Hyde Park went for Hoover, Landon, Willkie, and Dewey in the Roosevelt years. Chance meetings aren't awkward, however, because civility is the first law of gentility. When Kennedy ran against Henry Cabot Lodge their debates were almost courtly; they avoided such embarrassing proper nouns as Korea and McCarthy. Having confiscated Lodge's seat, Kennedy hit it off splendidly with his senatorial colleague from Massachusetts, Leverett Saltonstall, another fellow Cantab, and a Yale Democrat who ran against Saltonstall did so without the junior senator's support. Breeding rises above party. People with a great deal in common understand each other instantly, and can talk in shorthand. The President rarely makes friends quickly, yet he and McGeorge Bundy, his soft-spoken national security aide, were immediately congenial. "He and Mac come from the same background," a mutual friend explains. "*They* didn't know each other, but their *families* did."

Cultivated families admire elegance, and John Kennedy sets great store by good form. His circle doesn't include men who wear clocks on their socks, or call Shakespeare the Bard, or say budgetwise. "You know most of my friends have certain traits in common," he told Red Fay. "They don't smoke, they don't drink and they don't play poker. I didn't find these things out until I knew them; I just seem to be attracted by men like that. Maybe it's chemical." More likely it's social instinct. "He just doesn't like big fat guys or grouches," one of these friends observes. Neither does he like photographers who suggest that he pose in church, nor reporters who ask intimate questions, nor name-droppers. At a Hyannis Port party in the summer of 1961 a stranger kept referring familiarly to "Dick" Russell. The President left vexed. Afterward he explained, with some heat, "In the many years I've known him I've never called him anything but *Senator* Russell." Although he and Harold Macmillan chat frequently on the transatlantic telephone, they still address one another as "Mr. Prime Minister" and "Mr. President," and during Cabinet meetings Kennedy misters everyone except his brother. Toward the end of his Administration's first year an editor who was in his office heard him engage in three informal phone conversations with the Secretary of State. The

one of each was informal, but at the end of the third
alk the President said quietly, "Thank you, Mr.
Rusk."

The clarity of Mr. Rusk's prose was a major factor
n his appointment. Like all patricians, John Kennedy
ikes men of grace; someone who writes felicitously
s halfway home with him. At the height of the Ber-
in crisis of 1961 he received a letter from Charles
le Gaulle urging him not to negotiate. De Gaulle,
imself a Nichomachean gentleman, had put his
ase exquisitely. His coda began, "Upon what field
hall we meet?" An eloquent march of metaphors fol-
owed, demonstrating that in the writer's judgment
here was no proper field. The addressee, visibly ex-
ited, read it aloud to three friends. "Isn't that beauti-
ul?" he said at the end. "You agree with it?" asked
one of the listeners. "Oh, no!" the President said in-
tantly. "But what a marvelous style!"

Among the other requisites of Democratic Forsytes
eems to be the display of a few symptoms of Anglo-
philia. They all have a West End air, but none of
hem is a patch on the President. He has more than
ymptoms; he has a chronic case. Shipwrecked during
the war, he was found in the jungle by a native boy
who handed him a note from an allied agent. The
message opened ceremoniously, *On His Majesty's
Service*. Lieutenant Kennedy grinned. "You've got
to hand it to the British," he said to Ensign Barney
Ross, and afterward the lieutenant and the agent enjoyed a cup of tea together in the boondocks. Today

Kennedy's affection for that happy breed abides. I
is conspicuous in his reserve, the cut of his clothes
his fondness for understatement, his daughter's nurs
— Maude Shaw, a British nanny — and especially i
his reading habits. His favourite biographies ar
Cecil's *Melbourne*, Churchill's *Marlborough*, an
Duff-Cooper's *Talleyrand*, all by Britons. In th
White House he reads the English press as thoroughl
as American newspapers, poring over the *Spectator
Times, New Statesman, Economist*, and *Mancheste
Guardian Weekly*, and if one of them says somethin
beastly about him he will be stung, even though i
may have only a handful of subscribers in the Unite
States.

The President's menus aren't British, but they'r
not American, either. Harry Truman once calle
himself a meat-and-potatoes man. His Democrati
legatee is more of an oeufs-en-gelée-and-filet-mignon
with-sauce-Béarnaise-and-stuffed-artichokes man. I
this we see the fine Gallic hand of Jacqueline Bou
vier. Jacqueline honors a different prescript — their
was a sort of hands across the English Channel mar
riage — and she is partial to French food, Frencl
furniture, and French wine; during her husband'
senatorial days she used to tuck a bottle of wine i
his lunch hamper and send him packing off to th
Hill like a Hemingway hero.

Their tastes differ in other ways, because thei
backgrounds are different. The Kennedys are unique
Jacqueline, on the other hand, comes from a milie

which is familiar to any reader of the novels of F. Scott Fitzgerald, whose daughter is among the First Lady's friends. It is a world of estates with swimming pools, badminton courts, and stables, where little girls play under the eye of French governesses, are taught to dance with little boys in Eton jackets, and frequently learn to accept the fact that their parents are divorced. The charms of this environment are exaggerated. Since there is a felt need to be terribly chic, society tends to degenerate into café society, which is dreary, sterile, inbred. President Kennedy visited a Palm Beach New Year's Eve party, but the terribly chic newspaper there didn't mention it. The social idols of the hour were Porfirio Rubirosa, the Dominican playboy, and his wife Odile, so the paper ran a front-page picture of Odile doing the twist. Its editor explained, "We feel there are a lot of people just as important as the President."

The Gibbon of this twisting culture is Cholly Knickerbocker, alias Igor Cassini. The brother of the First Lady's dress designer, Cholly writes a Hearst column, and when Jacqueline Kennedy came out he named her the year's top debutante. She was an outstanding choice. As Cholly said archly, "You don't have to read a batch of press clippings to be aware of her qualities." Even so, society page editors riffled through her clippings with professional respect. Her father, John Vernon Bouvier III, was a stockbroker and a descendant of a Revolutionary War officer. There is a Bouvier Street in Philadelphia; there were Drexels in the family background. Jacqueline had attended Miss Chapin's School for the haughty in New York and had gone on to Miss Porter's School in Farmington, Connecticut, and to Vassar. She was a horsewoman, she wrote poetry on the side; *Vogue* became aware of her and so did *Life*.

Yet she is more than an ex-deb now. Jacqueline is no Eleanor Roosevelt, but she's not an Odile Rubirosa, either. Because she has a strong artistic bent she has moved from the trivial to the aesthetic, and is, in her *comme il faut* way, just as U as her husband. It was the impeccable Arthur Krock — Krock appears and reappears in the Kennedy saga, like a benign linking character in a Henry James novel — who persuaded the Washington *Times-Herald* to hire her as an Inquiring Camera Girl, and her fastidiousness has been endorsed by Russell Lynes.

Its quality is reflected in her redecoration of the Executive Mansion. "Of course I'm voting for Nixon," read a 1960 caption in the *New Yorker*, "but I can't help wishing I could see what Jackie would do with the White House." She was bound to do something; as the late Ike Hoover, a veteran White House usher, once observed, every First Family does everything as differently as possible from the one before. Still, there have been few changes of the guard so striking as 1961's. After the election the First Lady-Elect was itching to redecorate the house. If there is one thing a bluestocking hates it is fake antiques, and the public rooms of the White House were full of reproductions. The moment Mamie left, Jacqueline started heaving them out — along with the potted palms — and replacing them with the genuine article. Windows were opened, fireplaces were lighted for the first time in eight years, and McKinley's portrait was moved to a ground floor corridor.

Joe Kennedy, remembering the White House as it was in Roosevelt's time ("very cold"), remarked with his usual flinty detachment that his daughter-in-law had done a sensational job. Her television tour of the state rooms impressed a lot of dumb bastards who don't appreciate culture, though they might take exception to some of her ancillary activities. For she has done more than redecorate; the mansion has become a national home to creative Americans. Dwight Eisenhower, the painter, declared that he wasn't too certain what was art, but he knew what he liked, and Harry Truman, the pianist, said of something he didn't like that if it was art, he was a Hottentot. Jacqueline Kennedy, the connoisseur, makes both look like Hottentots, if not outright clods. She has a rare visual eye and is enthusiastic about all the fine arts, including the performing arts. As First Lady she encourages the Washington and New York ballets, the National Symphony, and the Washington Opera Society; the National Theater has a presidential box for the first time in forty years. She has introduced a series of concerts for children, and the mansion's East Room, which Abigail Adams used as a laundry and in which Theodore Roosevelt held a jujitsu exhibition, has under the Kennedys heard the anguish of *Macbeth,* the strains of Pablo Casals, and the thumps of Jerome Robbins's ballet troupe. If anyone mutters that these goings on are Frenchy, the hostess is insouciant. Where excellence is at stake, she won't give an inch to mass taste. She wants the best entertainment, the best appointments, the best personal appearance. Kenneth of Lilly Daché does her hair, and when she spoke to a group of farmers in a Venezuelan barnyard she wore an apricot dress and a coat of silk and linen sewed by Oleg Cassini.

Jacqueline is an eclectic blend of traditionalism and *ton.* In repose she evokes memories of young Edwardian ladies briefing themselves before a party by writing conversation topics on the sticks of a fan. In action she resembles a woman athlete. Really she is both. Most children of this century shed the past easily; they have little of it to shed. She comes from a class that has been bred to remember. At the same time, she has an exceptional sense of personal security and is, therefore, unafraid of innovation. Where Mary Lincoln wept because a gown was ruined, Jacqueline wears pedal pushers. But she has that uniformed nanny for Caroline. But she doesn't always use the nanny. She herself wheels a baby carriage, and round her neck she wears a classic, triple strand of pearls. The impression is of anomaly, as of a lovely mansion wired for sound. In her White House this is literally true. Moving to 1600 Pennsylvania Avenue, she surrounded herself with her own antiques and retainers

— meantime installing an intercom on the south porch to relay the cadence of John F. Kennedy, Jr.'s naptime breathing.

Since the inaugural Jacqueline's poetry has been appearing in fragments, like Emily Dickinson's. Recently a classmate unearthed a comic ode written for the classmate's wedding. It began by prophesying that the bride:

> *. . . in wedded bliss soon will be*
> *Vassar will miss her & so will we*
> *But watch yo' step honey on that path*
> *of roses*
> *There's mo' thorns 'neath them thar*
> *leaves than you Knowses . . .*

In her clear script Jacqueline drew a stark picture of six o'clock feedings and burnt toast, of the young wife envying "Jackie drinkin' Borbon at the Sorbon." Then the poetess peered into the far future, and prophecy ran amok:

> *Jackie skinny & underpaid*
> *Is earning her living as the French*
> *maid . . .*

Her Farmington yearbook noted that Jacqueline's ambition was "Not to be a housewife." She averted that, and without becoming a French maid, though she has encountered some rather prickly thorns of her own. While her role as cultural leader is agreeable, she is far less responsive to the nation's interest in her private life. In fact, she is probably the least enthusiastic company wife in the country. Her diffidence is so genuine that it is doubtful she grasped what lay ahead when she became engaged to the most eligible bachelor in Washington. The timing of every event seemed to be determined by the requirements of her husband's career — after a two-year courtship, their marriage had to await the adjournment of Congress in 1953 — and personal moments were observed by riptides of gaping mobs. She was aghast at the uninvited horde that showed up for the wedding, alarmed by the fingers that were forever plucking at her clothes. Most cruel was the summer of 1956, when Jack lost the Vice Presidential nomination. They had bought a $125,000 home in Virginia; she was expecting a child. Exhausted after the convention, Jack left to join his father abroad — and in his absence she lost her baby. The tragedy was duly noted in print, and the whole experience became such a nightmare that they sold the house, to Bobby and Ethel.

Glen Ora, the John Kennedys' house in Middleburg, Virginia, is a recent acquisition. To avoid the Pennsylvania Avenue showcase the First Lady spends much of her time there. Yet each time she goes, it is a news story. Her goldfish bowl grows more translucent all the time. No First Lady has been exposed to so blinding a glare of publicity since Frances Cleveland's picture was used, without authorization, to advertise a liver medicine. High school girls copy Jacqueline shamelessly; the length of her skirts, the dimensions of her form-fitting slacks, her preference for pink (sometimes called "hot pink") receive as much attention as all Katanga. And now she has a new worry. Caroline is a cynosure; people shout at her when she passes in a car, and she has begun to wonder why. Most mothers look forward to the day their first child will be able to read. This mother dreads it, for hers will be reading about herself. It's disconcerting enough to have small fry ogling the White House tennis courts and yelping, "You goofed, Jackie!" To find your little daughter a cover girl is far worse. Jacqueline's disapproval is good-humored — she calls herself Salinger's "greatest cross" — but it is also loud and clear. Recently a friend asked her how she liked an article about Caroline. She made a face. "Too cute," she said. "It made her sound like a spoiled brat." "Pierre liked it," the friend remarked, "and so did the President." She made another face and said tartly, "They're not very good judges, if you don't mind my saying so."

Curiosity about the First Family is inescapable. They entertain on the grand scale — Washington, in the President's words, is a much jazzier town these days. They are comely — a national campus poll in the spring of 1962 disclosed that American coeds feel their Chief Executive has more sex appeal than anybody, including Rock Hudson, and to men Jacqueline is a poster of beauty. Lastly, they have small children.

Wives gloat over bulletins describing Caroline's four-poster bed, the baby's white wicker bassinet, and the conversion of the White House solarium (where Eisenhower charcoal-broiled sirloin steaks) into a playroom. "You could see it was a great satisfaction to the people," Huckleberry Finn said of a piece of small news, "because naturally they wanted to know." They still do. No one should understand better than a former Inquiring Camera Girl, and women reporters, forced to rely on pre-inaugural photographs — which are dated by Caroline's baby fat — grumble about the "velvet curtain." But turnabout is not fair play. Jacqueline wasn't raised to be a newspaperwoman. She was brought up to be a lady, which isn't even the same thing as a First Lady. A lady is expected to be protective of the private I, like a scholar — like, say, young Jack Kennedy, whose shyness, though ruthlessly suppressed, may still be limned in President John Kennedy.

The President and his wife complement one another. Courting Jacqueline, he gave her biographies. She riposted with books she had illustrated. After their wedding she studied American history in Georgetown, the better to understand him, and since entering the mansion he has begun to share her regard for the fine arts. He is not conspicuously comfortable at White House soirées; frequently he turns the conversation to politics or slips away to run through his mail. All the same, he has come a long way. In his bedroom he has had high fidelity equipment installed, permitting him to hear classical records on Washington FM stations and revealing a preference unknown in his years of ascent, when, as someone said, his hunger for good music was satisfied by the swinging measures of "Hail to the Chief."

Jacqueline's mind is appreciative, his is inquiring. They meet in literature, for there is no author whose work is so remote that he cannot extract something from it. Among the writers who have been their guests at 1600 Pennsylvania Avenue are e. e. cummings as well as Barbara Ward, Robert Frost as well as Sir Charles Snow. Gore Vidal, another caller, suggested that the President examine *Coriolanus* for an earlier playwright's views of democracy, and the President and his wife read it aloud one foggy day at the Cape, although later, as Vidal remembers it, "He made the point with some charm that Shakespeare's knowledge of the democratic process was, to say the least, limited."

The anti-Shakespeare vote is rather large in parts of this country. Many a two-fisted American would be startled to learn what his chief had been up to. Those who know him merely wonder how he missed *Coriolanus* before. It's not like him to be so ill-read. He is the most literate President since Woodrow Wilson — F.D.R. talked to authors, he didn't read them — and when not writing his own books he has generally had his nose in somebody else's. "I've known him thirty years," says Lem Billings. "There has never been a moment when he didn't have something to read, and usually he has been working on at least two books at the same time." As a very young boy he was deep in James Fenimore Cooper. Bound for the South Pacific on a Navy transport he was either urging fellow officers to read his current favorites, Franz Werfel's *The Forty Days of Musa Dagh* and John Buchan's *Pilgrim's Way*, or poring over new finds; on Tulagi he read *War and Peace*, which is now among the volumes in the west sitting room. He was the chief senatorial patron of the Library of Congress, and after his presidential nomination he relaxed with Anthony Trollope. Today he complains that his literary diet is curtailed, yet recent examples of his general reading include George Kennan's *Russia and the West Under Lenin and Stalin*, Alan Moorehead's *The White Nile*, Henry A. Kissinger's *Necessity for Choice*, A. J. P. Taylor's *Origins of the Second World War*, Barbara W. Tuchman's *The Guns of August*, the historical novels of Mary Renault, and the thrillers of Ian Fleming.

There is such a thing as an intellectual profile. John Kennedy is too versatile to fit any palimpsested image, but this is one of the shadows he casts. He has always been attracted by ideas — during the war he kept a looseleaf notebook to record thoughts — and by the stimulus of debate. Red Fay remembers that in the Solomons Lieutenant Kennedy's Tulagi tent became "a world affairs forum, with the occupant as the moderator." He would cross foils with anyone, on almost any topic. He was silenced just once, and under the circumstances there wasn't much he could have said; a visiting Republican officer, not realizing who his antagonist was, bitterly denounced Roosevelt's appointment of wealthy ambassadors. Jim Reed, meeting Kennedy, instantly found himself in a verbal duel over Munich. Ensign Reed blamed Chamberlain; the lieutenant, Britain's marshmallow mood of the Thirties. "I came out second best," Reed recalls. "I didn't know he'd written a *book* about it."

As Richard Nixon discovered, Kennedy can quote other authors than himself. His bookishness is one of his debating strengths; he can bury an opponent in a cascade of facts. Even his conversation is studded with allusions, and he may be the only Hearst reporter ever to have cited Richard Brinsley Sheridan in a news story. In a single address he has quoted Wilson, Goethe, Faulkner, Artemus Ward, Finley Peter Dunne, Swift, Emerson, Lord Asquith, Tennyson, and Queen Victoria. His maiden speech in the Senate was so heavy it didn't make the New York *Times.* Since then he has learned the value of the offhand reference — reminding de Gaulle of Jefferson's and Franklin's affection for France, say, or twitting a convention of newspaper publishers by reminding them that Karl Marx was a correspondent for the New York *Tribune,* or casually revealing his familiarity with contemporary literature, as in his remarks after Hemingway's death.

Inevitably the induction of his Administration

brought a dramatic change in the official status of the literati. Under the old regime they had been outcasts. The Republicans did issue a cacophonous edict declaring that the party should "facilitate the utilization of friendly academicians in party affairs at all levels," but they didn't follow through practicewise. An Eisenhower Cabinet member inquired of *The Old Man and the Sea,* "Who would want to read a book about an old man who was a failure?" and Eisenhower himself declined to step into Sherman Adams's office and shake Robert Frost's hand. Kennedy's inaugural, on the other hand, was attended by some eighty invited artists, including W. H. Auden, Lewis Mumford, Allen Tate, and John Steinbeck, who in a hyperbolic mood expressed satisfaction that "literacy is no longer prima-facie evidence of treason."

If anything, scholarly achievement has become a requisite for appointees. A Mauldin cartoon depicted the new key to the capital — a Phi Beta Kappa key. As Truman admired generals and Eisenhower tycoons, Kennedy leans on fellow students. Among his advisers are some fifteen Rhodes scholars, led by the Secretary of State, and four professional historians. The Secretary of Defense, the Commissioner of Internal Revenue, the Chairman of the Civil Service Commission, and the ambassadors to India, Yugoslavia, and Japan are former college teachers. The President's expert on gold is a professor; so is the chief lieutenant of the Secretary of Agriculture, who is himself a member of Phi Beta Kappa. Even the Presilent's military adviser, General Maxwell D. Taylor, ame to him from the Lincoln Center for the Perform- ng Arts, and for the first time in history the White Iouse has a cultural coordinator, albeit a Yale man. The list of authors on the New Frontier is endless — t includes eight diplomats, four White House aides, he Solicitor General, the Assistant Secretary of State or International Affairs, the Deputy Assistant of State or Public Affairs, the Chief of the Disarmament Ad- ministration, the Chairman of the Council of Eco- nomic Advisers, the Postmaster General, and the At- orney General. Those who don't write read widely; Secretary Udall's private dining room is a haven for such Washington visitors as Arnold Toynbee. Udall's irst act upon assuming office was to study Harold Ickes's autobiography, and while in the office of the Secretary of the Treasury one may browse through a library which, during a recent call, included volumes by Churchill, Neustadt, Schlesinger, Galbraith, and, of course, a copy of *Profiles in Courage*.

If their leader weren't captain of the West, doubt- less he would be a member of the West's literary elite. His qualifications are gilt-edged: a Pulitzer Prize and original work which has been translated into Arabic, Japanese, Turkish, Vietnamese, Telegu, and Indone- sian. He wouldn't be an intellectual giant — his schol- arship is more persevering than illustrious — but he would be accepted, and he would find the company congenial, for he has more than a touch of artistic temperament. Like most writers, he is an insomniac.

His sleeplessness is not confined to periods of crisis
Sometimes he conducts routine business of the Fed
eral Government at odd hours; Lyndon Johnson and
Pierre Salinger are among those who have received
presidential calls after midnight. When he does drop
off, he's easily disturbed. One of his former room
mates found that Kennedy disliked the bed near the
window, so the roommate took it, which meant that
when he rose to use the bathroom at night he had to
tiptoe around Jack. No matter how softly he crept, a
lanky figure would heave up and snap, "God, can't
you stop the racket?"

Intellectuals are often nonconformists. Their early
school records may be unimpressive because as chil
dren they were indifferent to curricula — this was
true of Jack at Choate — though in the freer environ
ment of college they are likely to improve, as he did
in Cambridge. They are inclined to be impatient of
details; *e.g.*, orthography. Kennedy, like Fitzgerald,
became a popular author without mastering this ele
mentary skill. Despite his expensive boarding schools
he long wrote literary "litary," and as a Harvard
graduate he was capable of spelling peculiar "peci
liar." In the White House his handwritten memo
randa are usually correct, but occasionally he will
glance up from the paper and ask for help, and his
calligraphy has deteriorated. Handwriting speci
mens from his youth are quite legible, while presiden
tial communications have been returned to the man
sion with the baffled inquiry, "Who signed my letter?"

Details are unimportant because the litary man is reoccupied. At Choate, a classmate remembers, "the iggest complaints about him were that his room was ever neat and he was always late to classes." Before is marriage and his subsequent conversion into a ashion plate he would appear on Capitol Hill in haki trousers and mismated socks. For a time he arried candy to nibble between meals; Reed remembers the shocked look on the face of a hostess when Kennedy, engrossed in a dinner conversation, ignored he steak in front of him and absent-mindedly began popping caramels in his mouth. He is always leaving things behind, and though he should have learned ow to handle money years ago — he had a checking ccount in prep school and dabbled in stocks at Harard — he never seems to have any with him. His vartime crew, knowing that his family had plenty of noolah, thought it odd that he would put the bite n them until payday. After the war one veteran ame to Boston to help him politick. "I couldn't afford to be bouncing for different expenses," he recalls, but I found I was catching the tabs. It was the old tory. His pockets were empty. Then he flew West to ee me. I was watching every penny — making three undred a month and a child on the way. Well, he lidn't have a cent. I had to give him twenty dollars to et on the plane. I said, listen, I want this back, I eed it. Of course, I got it." Senator George Smathers, Southern Democrat who is one of the President's ocial friends, got his back on a European trip by picking up *all* the tabs and later sending his amnesic companion a bill for half.

Bobby Kennedy attributes this trait to their parents' deliberate de-emphasizing of the family fortune. "Mother impressed on us the value of nickels, dimes, and quarters," he says, "but we were never conscious of wealth. The opposite was preached constantly, so we forget about money. For example, I didn't bring any with me today. I just didn't think about it. He's the same way." Yet Bobby isn't distracted in other ways. The President is. The Attorney General's comb is always within reach, but during the 1960 campaign his older brother borrowed combs, and even pencils, from the press.

Theodore H. White, the historian of that election, wrote that at times "following him was like attending a peripatetic and anecdotal course in American history." The candidate was campaigning and lecturing at the same time. He was also studying; his preparation for the first debate with Nixon resembled nothing so much as a pre-exam cram session. Like all scholars he enjoys the learning process, and his old school tie holds him fast. The library housing his presidential papers will be in Cambridge. When he defended the electoral college, Professor Holcombe marshaled his arguments for him. Asked by the Senate to chair the committee which would pick America's five greatest deceased senators (they were to be Clay, Webster, Calhoun, La Follette, and Taft), he turned to his old faculty for advice. And it is significant that two of the

President's three favorite pundits — Walter Lippmann, Joseph Alsop, and James Reston — are Harvard men. (The odd man is Reston, who went to some
school out West.)

In the fall of 1961 John F. Kennedy, Jr., could be
observed wriggling in the back of a Hyannis Port station wagon, wearing a crimson sweater with a tiny H
on it. "Of all the boys Jack likes Harvard best," Joe
Kennedy said then. "Bobby and Teddy don't care for
it much, and I guess I have the old Boston prejudice
against it. But it means a lot to him." How much it
meant had been revealed earlier that year, when approximately one-third of all first-rank appointments,
including four Cabinet posts, went to old wearers of
the Crimson. His *Alumni Bulletin* depicted the White
House with an enormous Harvard banner draped
across the front. "Harvard men," the President's former government teacher observed cheerfully, "are
clearly entitled to have faith in the new Cabinet."

There is irony here. Harvard, like Shakespeare and
ballet troupes, provokes uneasy stirrings among the
electorate. A Saltonstall or a Lodge couldn't indulge
himself so. Kennedy can, because it is so hard to credit
highbrow bias in a Boston Irish Catholic. "Jack's Catholicism is the very thing that has brought him into
prominence," Schlesinger told Joe McCarthy, bi-
ographer of the Kennedy family, before the election.
"Looking as Jack does and talking as he does, a liberal minded senator from New England who went to
Choate School and comes from a wealthy family —

if he were just another Protestant, nobody would pa
much attention to him." Having passed the religiou
test, the President is now free to embrace institution
considered antithetical to the Irish. Thus the Roscom
mon myth is an asset; John Kennedy can elevate me:
who, under Adlai Stevenson, would have been score:
as "eggheads," and his wife can blithely follow he
class instincts, even to presenting him with a pin:
hunting jacket, which won hardly any votes in Eas
Boston.

Honey Fitz never rode to hounds, read the *Econo
mist,* or hung around violoncellists. "Sweet Adeline'
and popcorn in Fenway Park were good enough fo
Honey, which may be the reason Lodge, Sr., licked
him. For a democratic country the United States i:
highly susceptible to well-heeled candidates. Shortl}
after Harriman's election to the governorship of Nev
York he was asked whether America should be run by
a wellborn elite, and he instantly replied, "Yes, if they
can get elected." Nowadays they get elected often
Kennedy beat Nixon, the man who had come up the
hard way, and many people believe Nelson Rockefeller, with Mrs. Rockefeller, could have taken them
both. In a stable, competitive society, the discreet
patrician has total status. He is acceptable everywhere — as, in a revolutionary society, he would be
acceptable nowhere. During the 1950's, a Massachusetts politician told Joe McCarthy, "If you had a Kennedy sticker on your car it meant that you were mix-

ng with the right people." In the 1960's smart fashion models remake themselves to look like Jacqueline, because that is what their clients want. "The President and his wife," Edwin A. Roberts wrote in the *Wall Street Journal*, "are regarded somewhat like Hollywood heroes, a golden couple with absolutely everything a world can offer and loved because of it."

Honey, who died in 1950, would have enjoyed his grandson's success, though he might have flinched at some of the implications. John Kennedy's career bears a striking resemblance to that of a member of the Establishment. The word is rarely heard in this country. It means the ruling class to educated Englishmen, whom young Jack first encountered in large numbers during his late, impressionable adolescence. The ambassador was a real ambassador then, and while he was cutting a swath in the Court of St. James (by typically refusing to wear satin knee pants), his children mixed with the pukka London gentry. Jack's favorite sister Kathleen ("Kick") joined it permanently, marrying the Marquess of Hartington. The marquess died in France fighting with the Coldstream Guards, and later Kick was killed in a plane crash while en route to the Riviera, but the ties remain, relating the President by marriage to David Ormsby-Gore, the British ambassador in Washington and, more distantly, to Harold Macmillan. Ormsby-Gore is in addition an old acquaintance of John Kennedy's. During the late 1930's the future President was commuting between Harvard and the

United Kingdom, and he made lasting friendship among the toffs. It is a sardonic footnote to Sinn Fein ism that when he visited Patrick Kennedy's Wexfor County birthplace, he was accompanied by an Eng lish lady. Afterward she remarked — to her escort' dismay — "That was just like Tobacco Road."

The American Establishment is more elusive than Britain's. Here it is a concept rather than a club, and no two sociologists are in accord on its membership list. Writing in the *American Scholar*, Richard H Rovere concludes that while John Kennedy belongs he is not of the "Inner Circle" — as, for example Dean Rusk is. Kennedy himself takes the position that every President is an ex-officio Establishmentarian. The office excepted, however, he doubts his eligibility. Rocking thoughtfully he says, "I'm of the Establishment in the sense of where I've lived, and my schools, but in the sense of the Anglo-Saxon Establishment — no. When I go into the N.A.M. I get a pretty cold reception; they're not very sympathetic. You really have to be a Republican to be a member. Of course, Nixon doesn't belong, but Rockefeller is the epitome of it. In my case, my politics and my religion are against it. If the Democratic party had an Establishment candidate, it was Stevenson."

Yet Catholicism apart — and it was set apart on November 8, 1960 — the President's social values are indistinguishable from Stevenson's. Every cultural anthropologist who has scrutinized the Establishment agrees that the New York *Times* is at the core of it.

"The *Times*," Rovere writes, "has no close rival as an Establishment voice." It is a voice to which Kennedy continually harks. "I've seen him leaf through that paper looking for criticism," says a friend who visits him weekends. "Ninety per cent will be favorable, but he tortures himself, seeking out the rest." This, as a *Times* leader would say, is not without significance. The President doesn't feel that way about the Chicago *Tribune*, despite its circulation. He is as devoted to New York's Old Gray Lady as the late George Apley was to the late Boston *Transcript*, and his fidelity is of long standing. Lem Billings recalls that when they met at Choate in 1931, fourteen-year-old Jack Kennedy was a *Times* subscriber — "the only subscriber that age I knew, and he read every word of it." The President feels that the Lady's editorial page sermons are as weighty as *Times* news is thorough, an attitude explicable only on Establishmentarian grounds. Salinger keeps telling him that the paper reaches a limited audience. A political scientist reports, "I've said to him, 'Look. The *Times* has one following, the *Courier-Journal* a second, the San Francisco *Chronicle* a third. You have to get this thing in perspective.'" It doesn't matter. What counts is that the subscription list of the *Times* includes John F. Kennedy, Choate '35, and an old boy wants the good opinion of his compeers.

The rules of traditional aristocracy are very firm on one point: the great leap to acceptance may not be made in one generation. Certain privileges and tokens of recognition are withheld from the self-made man, but are available to his scions. Joe's public service under three Presidents notwithstanding, he was never granted an honorary degree by Harvard. His son the senator was so invested in 1956, and is an overseer of the university. The way had been paved by the father, first with a generous crust of precious metals. The ambassador resolved all conceivable financial problems while his children were still children. He gave each an initial trust fund of over a million dollars, putting them in a position where they "could spit in my eye." As John Jacob Astor III used to say, a man who has a million dollars is as well off as if he were rich. With the maturing of subsequent trust funds, the assets of the young Kennedys have multiplied, and today the President is rich even by Astor standards. At the time he took office he was worth about ten million dollars, all of it in government bonds. Sixteen months later, when he passed his forty-fifth birthday, he received half again as much, and still more will come to him when he is fifty. His present trust income, after taxes, is in the neighborhood of a hundred thousand dollars a year.

In his school days the family wealth permitted him to see the world before he joined the Navy, and, more important, it paid for a lot of Back Jack handbills later. One of the untaught facts of political life is that running for President costs lots of money. Any man infected with Potomac Fever must somehow lay his hands on a large supply of cash. He can inherit it —

in *Six Crises* Richard Nixon predicts that soon only heirs of wealthy men may be candidates — or he can make himself attractive to the well-heeled, as Nixon himself did. There is no third way. Post-convention bills are enormous, and for a man who is compelled to fight his way to the convention through primaries, as Kennedy was, the total bill is staggering. Long before his nomination he was spending seventy thousand dollars a year out of his pocket for his Washington office; the budget for a single banquet was two thousand dollars. Barnstorming the nation, he bought his own plane — with his mileage it was cheaper than commercial flights — and on Election Day 1960 Hyannis Port was outfitted with four teletypes and thirty new phones, many of them direct lines. The long distance tab that night was estimated at ten thousand dollars. In the G.O.P. these disagreeable details are handled by assorted Maecenases; the predicament of the Democrats explains their affection for candidates with private troves. Someone must pay the ransoms of ambition, and in Jack Kennedy's case the someone worked diligently in New York, at 230 Park Avenue, behind a ninth floor door which bears in bold letters the name of Joseph P. Kennedy.

The father gave his son much more than cash, however. Long ago he created a soil — some would say a hothouse — in which exotic shoots could flourish. This setting has determined the direction of John Kennedy's life at countless little junctures. If it had been less plush, for instance, he would never have gone into PT's. In the early months of World War II the Motor Torpedo Boat command was looking for youths with yachting experience — a select class. The cadre they recruited was bound to be atypical. There was Ensign Paul G. Pennoyer, Jr., for example, a grandson of J. P. Morgan. And there was Kennedy, who had sailed on a championship crew at Harvard, and who spied his first PT while in Martha's Vineyard at the helm of his own sloop.

Later the politician was to find his patriciate friends immensely useful. Intelligent, educated, and independent, they could leave their paneled offices and cotillions and pitch in when he needed able campaign executives. From the Bellevue Hotel to the White House, he has been surrounded by men who have given his career an elegant, mandarin tone. "In 1960 we all took leaves of absences from our offices and started out in Wisconsin," Billings says. "There were ten districts in that first state, and we took over four of them. I had the third, Lacrosse. Then there was Ben Smith — he had the tenth — and Ted Reardon and Chuck Spalding. We picked up momentum in West Virginia, and when we reached Nebraska, Rip Horton joined us." Reardon and Smith went to Harvard, Spalding to Yale; Ralph Horton, like Billings himself, is a Princetonian. Year after year they and a dozen others have given Kennedy the old Ivy college try. The fact that several hold vital offices in his Washington is unsurprising. His loyalty to them is as strong as ethnic bonds were to his grandfather. No one calls them cronies — though that is what they really are — because it is generally felt that their service is a bargain for the government. In Sargent Shriver's phrase they are "blue-chip men," the very kind of public servants that Administrations attempt, usually with small success, to lure to the capital.

Their role tends to overshadow the part which older men of power have played in Kennedy's life. For years patroons of the ambassador's generation were patrons of his son. The ambassador never hesitated to make this claim on his friends; at every turning point in Jack's early life some member of the U.S. Establishment was waiting to greet him and, if necessary, to help him. Based in Florida as a junior naval officer, he discussed public affairs with James Cox, the Democratic presidential candidate of 1920. Discharged from the Navy, he was appointed special correspondent by William Randolph Hearst. Arriving in the lower house of Congress, he inherited Arthur Krock's Negro valet, and when he moved into the upper house he became Herbert Hoover's "favorite Democratic Senator."

The political advantage of these contacts is questionable. They brought no new support to the candidate or his party. Their educative value, on the other hand, is incalculable. Wherever Jack went, he saw the seats of authority at close range. On one prewar trip his hosts were Bill Bullitt in Paris, Tony Biddle in Warsaw, and Chip Bohlen in Moscow. And while still an undergraduate he himself knew the solemnity of responsibility. The Nazis sank a British liner, and his father sent him to Glasgow to handle the problem of American survivors. Thus Jack became a cosmopolite — though scarcely a socialite — and turned out a best seller about the gathering storm, for which one of Joe's friends suggested a title and an agent, while another, Henry Luce, wrote the foreword. Declared Luce: "If John Kennedy is characteristic of the younger generation — and I believe he is — many of us would be happy to have the destinies of the Republic turned over to his generation at once."

But the author of *Why England Slept* wasn't characteristic. The representative American of twenty-three hadn't watched a bullfight or climbed Mt. Vesuvius, hadn't met Cardinal Eugenio Pacelli, hadn't chatted with Franklin Roosevelt and Winston Churchill and couldn't, for that matter, have coaxed the publisher of *Time* into writing an introduction to his first manuscript. All these came to pass because the ambassador had passed the word along. That he should have done so is not strange. Nor is it odd that the beneficiary of so extensive a preparation should become a polished leader. The remarkable thing is that he should ever have become identified with an oppressed minority, and that this, indeed, should have been the key issue in his bid for national power. Somehow our electoral system works, but the American voter moves in a mysterious way, his wonders to perform.

THREE

Sort of Sideways

I<small>N A QUIET</small> office at 1701 K Street, far from the madding press club, is Arthur Krock. Courtly, courteous, surrounded by classics and honorary degrees, he contemplates Washington with a lofty eye. Here in the capital Krock's position is quasi-judicial. If his manner these days is also a trifle paternal, it should be remembered that he was a Washington correspondent seven years before John Kennedy was born, and that his perspective on the Kennedy Presidency is unique.

"I've known him since he was a little boy. I titled his first book" — he displays his copy, with a worshipful inscription signed *Jack Kennedy*. "When he was broken up during the war I sent him out to J. G. F. Speiden's Arizona ranch to recuperate, and when he came down here as freshman congressman and was invited to the White House, I asked him to give me accounts of what happened. I've still got those reports — long, detailed, typed — very good. Then I was on the Pulitzer board, and I worked as hard as I could to get him that prize. He is intelligent. And he certainly has courage; there's no doubt of that. But —"

But Krock is saturnine. The New Frontier does not enchant him. His ties to the First Family — he wistfully recalls escorting Jacqueline Bouvier to her first Gridiron tea — merely make his gloom harder to bear. The whole business reminds him of the Thirties, when he felt obliged to return dire verdicts against another old friend, from Hyde Park. There was no helping it then, there is none now. Krock calls presidential shots as he sees them, and his is a conservative eye.

"As a candidate he hit Eisenhower for indecisiveness, for lack of candor, for failure to use the full powers of his office," he says of Kennedy. "Well, he has repeated every one of the errors of weaknesses he attributed to Eisenhower. Take Cuba. He was indecisive there. You can't blame his advisers; the ultimate responsibility was his." Krock lights a cigar and draws deeply. "I'm doubtful that we did the best we could in selecting this President. I have grave reservations, although really neither he nor Nixon was big enough for the job. No one could be. The difficulties that Kennedy saw in 1960 are inherent in the office."

If any Washingtonian is immune to panoply, it is Arthur Krock. Yet there is more to the Presidency than the incumbent. Like the New York *Times,* it is an institution. And when it is seen in its institutional light, even a Krock is dazzled. A few nights earlier he watched the John Kennedys on television. "I had to pinch myself," he says. "They've been transformed. They're exalted, they have a presence. *That's* the office, too."

The office does more for some than for others. There is no clear relationship between the degree of exaltation and the judgment of history — the Roosevelts had immense presence and are still regarded highly, but Warren Harding, our worst Chief Executive, was one of the most popular. All the same, it is clear that the Presidency brought Kennedy far more new support than anyone had anticipated. For almost a decade opinion samplers had reported that Dwight Eisenhower was the man most Americans admired. On the first anniversary of the Kennedy inaugural they found that Ike's successor had succeeded him here, too. To his uncritical admirers the young President has an irresistible charisma. "I believe in anything he believes in!" a woman gasped after one of his public appearances, and once when he went for a stroll on the south grounds of the White House two passing motorists, each cheering him, collided.

At times the First Family seems to dominate the newspapers. During his campaign Kennedy had repeatedly declared that he was tired of getting up every morning and reading what Khrushchev and Castro were doing; he wanted to know what the President of the United States was doing. Several months after moving into the new mansion he remarked dryly to Sorensen that "Some people are tired of getting up every morning and reading what Kennedy is doing. They want to read what Khrushchev and Castro are doing." They didn't really. Watching the President had become an opiate of the masses, and it was accompanied by a kind of Nell Gwyn crush — a Kennedy barber, swamped with requests for tufts of his hair, was asked didn't he think it all ridiculous; his shy reply was that he had taken some home to his wife. Only the Capitol, Washington's high ground, was inaccessible to the tide. John Kennedy was too familiar a figure on the Hill; one senator said tartly, "He is just someone who used to sit beside me — when he happened to be here." Nevertheless, even there Representative Hale Boggs was overheard early in 1962 advertising the fact that he had received a letter from the President "in his own handwriting."

There is nothing novel about this enthusiasm. It is the very stuff of leadership. A man must kindle it to win high office, and the qualities that put him there tend to increase the public's affection. Let a new tenant move into the White House and his followers exaggerate his every virtue. Grant's distaste for red tape was the talk of the Seventies; Coolidge's laconism, the marvel of the Twenties. The public resolves that a Chief Executive shall gain in stature, so he does. Those who have known him before regard him as a stranger. Waiting outside Franklin Roosevelt's office Norman Thomas said to Raymond Fosdick, "Ray, that fellow in there is not the fellow we used to know. There's been a miracle here." Similarly, Barney Ross says of John Kennedy, "The big difference in him is, he's grown while the rest of us have stood still. He's deeper, more mature, more intellectual. Out there in the Pacific we were equal. Now all of us, all his old friends, hold him in awe." Ross grins. "Of course, how much of that is the Presidency, I don't know. It *does* have an aura."

A new President's former colleagues begin to dote on him, and some of them go so far as to ape him. Bess Furman noticed that everyone around Roosevelt laughed the same way he did — "a little toss-back of the head, then all-out, tooth-displaying mirth." Kennedy's first mimic was Ted Sorensen. Even before the election Sorensen was being called the boss's alter ego: "When Jack is wounded," reporters said, "Ted bleeds." He had picked up his chief's mannerisms, his writing style, his thought processes. A friend of the Kennedys' watched him and blurted out, "Say, you're more like Jack than Jack himself." Sorensen looked disturbed — as would any man whose identity is threatened. The blurter remembers that Jack drew him aside. "Don't," he ordered. "He gets that from all sides." Today Sorensen has lots of company. Recently Red Fay was addressing an audience. "In the middle of the speech," he says, "I realized I had the old head cocked to the right; the left hand going, stabbing the air, making a point; and the other hand level, sawing air." A few weeks later Pierre Salinger did precisely the same thing over a Kansas City television station. The instant he left the studio someone taunted him about it, though he had been unaware of imitating anyone. Some people think Caroline has begun to hunch her shoulders like her father, and certainly there are scores of men in Washington who have unconsciously adopted the Kennedy pause, the Kennedy walk, and the Kennedy habit of disciplining a shock of unruly hair — even when they haven't got unruly hair or, for that matter, hair.

What is extraordinary about all this is the President's reaction to it. He observes the tributes paid to him almost as though they were meant for someone else. His self-possession isn't as majestic as that of the dying Webster — "Wife, children, doctor, I trust on this occasion I have said nothing unworthy of Daniel Webster" — but without using the third person he does convey a third-person air. This objectivity gives him a certain tactical edge with people. It permits him to edit his professional friendships dispassionately — some say ruthlessly. Few politicians have been able to rise so rapidly without incurring massive political debts. Apart from the Attorney General and the Secretary of Health, Education, and Welfare, his strongest campaign backers are absent from his Cabinet, which includes two former governors of small political caliber, an ex-congressman, two Republicans, and — as Secretary of State — an inactive Democrat whose pre-convention choice was Adlai Stevenson. In choosing his ministers the President's only traditional standard was geographic distribution. Appointments weren't made to meet any election commitment. He didn't even think about them until he had become President-Elect. He assumes most men support him out of conviction, not for payola. Their faith in him neither surprises nor elates. It is simply there, like the Washington Monument. Discovering an incompetent appointee on a lower level he demanded, "What's he doing in the government?" "He admired you so much," he was told. "His imagination was fired by your eloquence in the campaign, your dedication, your vision." Most leaders would have been warmed, if only momentarily, by this intimation of magnetic appeal. This one nodded shortly. "Yes, that happens," he said flatly, "but now would you please explain what he's doing in the government?"

Obviously such an attitude is instinctive. If he had not had it, it would not have been possible to invent it. And indeed, detachment has run through his forty-five years like a lonely thread. Motoring through Europe with Lem Billings the summer after his freshman year at Harvard, he was intent upon taking each nation's pulse. The car was his, and he would give a lift

to any hitchhiker to quiz him in pidgin about attitudes toward aggression, hopes for peace, faith in the
Maginot Line. What impressed Billings most was that
Kennedy was seldom offended by anyone, even when
offense was intended. At Vesuvius two German soldiers they had picked up secretly decided to beat
them to the top. The Americans, opting for the gentler
of the two slopes, were greeted at the summit by their
crowing guests. Billings thought this rude. Kennedy
merely made a note about the Teutonic will to win.
Again, in Munich, they learned that the great tourist
stunt was to drink a stein of beer outside the Hofbrau
House and then slip away with the stein. It was all
good fun, and a Nazi there told them how to do it.
They were quite taken by the man. Despite his brown
shirt he was well educated, spoke English with an Oxford accent, and seemed to be going out of his way to
be genial. They followed his plan — and were instantly caught. As a waiter stopped Billings and re-
trieved the stein from under his coat, they turned
and beheld their brown-shirted planner laughing de-
risively. He had deliberately trapped them. Billings
was enraged, but Kennedy, unruffled, merely made
another quiet note, this time about Nazi treachery.

"Emotions move people far more strongly than
facts," he observed unemotionally, chronicling the
collapse of the prewar West, and to his father he
wrote -- during the agony of the German blitz — "I
of course don't want to take sides too much." His personal destiny has been treated as impersonally.

"What do you want to do?" he asked his PT crew as they swam around the sinking hulk of their boat. "I have nothing to lose." Eleven years later, when he lay critically ill after an operation, his father was struck by his fatalistic attitude. Either he would die or he wouldn't, he said; there wasn't much he could do about it. At one point during the hectic vice-presidential nomination of 1956, he appeared to have won. The whole country was in a sweat. Sorensen held out his hand to congratulate him, but Kennedy, calmly dressing in front of a television screen like an Ingmar Bergman character, replied, "No, not yet." On election night four years later, in front of another television set, Jacqueline Kennedy said, "Oh, Bunny, you're President now!" With the objectivity of a commentator he reported to her that it was too early to tell. Antagonists are judged by the same unbiased eye. In that 1956 convention his rebuff was widely attributed to the floor strategy of the present Speaker of the House, a Massachusetts Democrat but no friend. "If McCormack wanted to put the knife in me, he had every right to do so," Kennedy said neutrally. "That's politics." And in that 1960 triumph, when his staff fumed because Richard Nixon postponed his admission of defeat, he told them, "Why should he concede? I wouldn't."

Deep in the man is a sense of autonomy, a capacity to view all society extrinsically. Kennedy enthusiasts attribute his presidential victory to political genius; with chilly realism he observes that a switch here, a switch there, and the genius would be named Nixon. One of his favorite phrases is "in my judgment." His judgment is unlike anyone else's. He ignores people whom the world esteems, values people the world ignores, and sorts them out according to their talents. To a remarkable degree his friendships are compartmentalized. They include a number of men who would like to shoot one another on sight. In Congress he was on pleasant terms with Vito Marcantonio, John Rankin, Paul Douglas, and Barry Goldwater. In the White House his personal, political, and social allies rarely mix. Sorensen continues to be very close to him. Their relationship is almost telepathic. In the West Wing they anticipate one another and need scarcely speak as they work together, disposing of administrivia. But this is an office association; after hours they rarely see each other. At the same time, Kennedy's social acquaintances tend to be apolitical, and his literary acquaintances to be apolitical and asocial. If a man's convictions conflict with his role, he checks them at the door. John Sherman Cooper is a Republican senator. He comes to 1600 Pennsylvania Avenue not as a Republican, however, but as a friend.

"Don't take down a fence until you know why it was put up," Robert Frost wrote. John Kennedy likes that line. For him good fences make a good Presidency. He erects them between people, and between problems. The day the Russians announced that they would resume nuclear testing he was talking to a

Washington correspondent. Mac Bundy entered the room with the news. The Chief Executive listened intently — and went on with the interview. Again, this writer was in the oval study when word of Sam Rayburn's fatal illness reached the President. He crossed his study to take the call. Clearly he was moved, and he said so. Then he replaced the receiver in its cradle, returned to his rocker, and, after rocking in silence for a moment, resumed the conversation.

We were discussing *Why England Slept,* his description of how England slept through appeasement, which sold eighty thousand copies twenty-two years ago and was reissued last fall. Reappraising it he displayed the same aloofness: "I dipped into it recently. Parts of it were heavy going. I don't know whether people would be interested in it now." He was reminded of a prescient passage in the book, describing Russian disarmament proposals of the Thirties as propaganda devices, and he nodded thoughtfully, as though acknowledging a point in behalf of an absent author. "Yes, parts of it are relevant today," he conceded. "Of course, they could take nuclear disarmament now, because they have conventional weapons." He reflected again and made a counter point: the study was dated. "You know, the League experience is not encouraging," he concluded. "They had the best chance we've had, because there was no bitterness; Hitler wasn't strong yet."

The absent writer — gangling young Jack Kennedy, snub-nosed and tense — sounded several notes in 1940 which are familiar in the 1960's: the need to sacrifice during crises, to avoid public scapegoats, and to keep isms out of Latin America; and the importance of voluntary restraint in an independent press. His book drew another conclusion which is important in understanding the man he was to become. It dealt with one of the most vexing dilemmas in contemporary politics, the short-run advantages of totalitarian governments over republics. Although "freedom from centralized authoritarianism" is one of democracy's great cornerstones, he wrote, that very liberty can threaten national security. Regimented people can be told what to do; free people must be won over, and the winning takes time. Quoting Sir Stanley Baldwin, who estimated the lag between a democracy and a dictatorship at two years, Kennedy blamed the inertia of that era on the British public. Then, broadening his indictment, he charged that the United States had also been "asleep at the switch." Later this concept grew on him, and he was reminded of, and discomforted by, the contest between Sparta and Athens. In the Tulagi tent debates, Fay recalls, "he had a strong feeling that we were fighting in that God-forsaken place because we, the voters, had failed to see the issues clearly. He said that as citizens we all held office, and that we hadn't done a very good job of meeting our responsibilities."

That, really, is the theme of *Profiles in Courage*. Kennedy's political heroes had to be heroic because their constituents weren't as farsighted as they were; each leader had to choose between a surrender of principle and disregard for what Thomas Hart Benton called "the bubble of popularity that is won without merit and lost without crime." When *Profiles* was published the author told a Harvard audience that elected representatives are forever "dragging the anchor of public opinion." He didn't despise the anchor. It was there, it had to be moved. He simply observed that as long as a politician is attached to it he cannot "with dexterity slip from position to position," as, he added pointedly, the scholar can.

Today Kennedy the politician-scholar compares the Nazi threat of twenty-five years ago with the Soviet menace today. He has called America's 1950's "the years the locust have eaten," the very phrase Sir Stanley used to describe Britain's 1930's. Completing the figure, Dwight Eisenhower would be our Neville Chamberlain and John Kennedy our Winston Churchill — unless Eisenhower were Baldwin, in which case the umbrella would go to Kennedy. Really the comparison of eras is little more than a historian's game. It has some validity; America now, like England then, has been indolent, complacent, unaware. The difficulty is that cold war, unlike war, doesn't generate much heat at home. Although the President has sounded calls to action, the alarm bell seems muted. As Joe Kennedy wrote four years before the publication of *Why England Slept*, "Americans are not easily stirred to action. The spectacle must be dramatic. The movie is worthless unless it is at least colossal." A Chief Executive's command is worthless unless it is at least Churchillian. If the presidential trumpet gives an uncertain sound, only Ted Sorensen will prepare himself to the battle.

John Kennedy hasn't changed course. The twentieth-century challenge to democratic resourcefulness is still very much on his mind. "He mentions it all the time," says Salinger. "That," says Sorensen, "is one of the reasons he sought the Presidency. He felt that people needed to grasp the nettle." Presidents, however, can be just so forceful. A free society exercises continual restraints upon them. Musing over the problem of meeting Russian thrusts he says, "There *are* advantages to centralized power." He casually cites a luncheon at which he tried to induce network executives to release material for the United States Information Agency. "In Russia that would be no problem," he says wryly. "It wouldn't even be a matter for thought." Reminded that Harry Truman called presidential power the power to persuade, he nods vigorously and comments, "Yes, that's it."

Since Baldwin's day — even since Truman's — the problem has acquired a new shape. A President may issue bold executive orders, which makes things easier. But he must act in concert with other chiefs of state, which makes them much harder. "Everything is different now," Bobby Kennedy remarks. "The lag isn't two years any more. We can move more quickly.

Yet democracy is still more cumbersome than dictatorship. If this were a dictatorship the President could grind out stuff day after day, as Khrushchev can. Even answering Khrushchev is a problem; England thinks we should talk, France not. The President must consult his allies — and Fulbright and Dirksen — and at the same time keep his own house in order. One of our chief allies may agree to a proposal only if Country X approves of it. Another will agree only if Country X isn't even informed of it. This requires a mastery of politics not even contemplated twenty years ago."

A nineteenth-century Frenchman had his suspicions, though. "It is chiefly in foreign relations," Alexis de Tocqueville wrote a hundred and twenty-five years before Kennedy's election, "that the executive power of a nation finds occasion to exert its skill and strength. If the existence of the Union were perpetually threatened, if its chief interests were in daily connection with those or other powerful nations, the executive department would assume increased importance in proportion to the measures expected of it and to those which it would execute." In the Sixties that waxing importance is felt everywhere. Asked at the inaugural what Europe expected of America's new President, a man fresh from there replied, "Too much." The President himself sums up his diplomatic position in those first weeks: "I was new to the world scene. I succeeded Eisenhower, who was known and whose position was clear. Naturally there was some curiosity about me. Also, I was young, and most of the men I would be dealing with were older."

He satisfied their curiosity with a technique de Tocqueville couldn't have foreseen: the personal confrontation. Kennedy summitry began almost at once; in the first ten months of his Administration he held seventy-five meetings with other chiefs of state, and despite the commotions of his second presidential spring he turned aside to entertain such obscure visiting firemen as Cameroun's Ahmadou Ahidjo, Togo's Sylvanus Olympio, and His Beatitude Makarios III, President of Cyprus. On the whole, these confrontations have been a success. Though they later found bones to pick with him, even Charles de Gaulle and Konrad Adenauer were impressed. De Gaulle remarked that in his entire life he had encountered only two genuine statesmen, and one of them was Kennedy; Adenauer, de Gaulle's other choice, announced as he departed the Executive Mansion, "I've never left this house feeling better." Communists felt worse, because the President's footwork was so much faster than theirs. To the proverb-quoting Russians he was proverbial — "You have offered to trade us an apple for an orchard. We don't do that in this country." — and he pointedly told Nikita Khrushchev that he hoped Khrushchev would be able to keep his Lenin Peace Prize. Even when Kennedy skidded he seemed to keep his footing. His Canadian visit disclosed that his French hadn't improved a bit since his 1937 trip with Billings, so he turned it to his advantage — by comparing it with Prime Minister John Diefenbaker's.

"He was so much better prepared than Diefenbaker and Macmillan that it was embarrassing," a witness to those conferences observes. His youth, it had been predicted, would put him at a strategic disadvantage in conclaves. Yet foreign secretaries are as struck by his talent for the specific as office secretaries, and so are their chiefs. Among those who have taken his measure and then commented upon this circumstantial gift are Macmillan, David Ben-Gurion, Willy Brandt, Hayato Ideka of Japan, Modibo Keita of Mali, Mohammed Ayub Khan of Pakistan, and Achmed Sukarno of Indonesia and the Greater East Asia Co-Prosperity Sphere. "Your President," Britain's Prime Minister murmured, "catches on to ideas very fast." Ben-Gurion had expected oratory. Instead the President led him into a room, closed the door, and regaled him with statistics about Israel. Ideka wondered where all the aides and *aides mémoire* were. He seemed to be alone with this one man, this rocking encyclopedia on the Far East. But the widest eyes were those of Willy Brandt. Most Americans are familiar with Willy's office, mayor of West Berlin. Few are aware that there is also a mayor of *East* Berlin, whose father, Friedrich Ebert, was the first president of the Weimar Republic. Their own President not only knew it; he knew more than his guest about the man. "I couldn't answer some of his questions," Willy confessed at lunch immediately after his baptism of facts. "He asked me whether Ebert's other son was also a Communist. Ebert's other son! I didn't even know he *had* another son!"

The success of these Information Please blitzes demonstrates that political and diplomatic arts really aren't so far apart. Larry O'Brien, a Massachusetts Hibernian who did not grow up on the Kennedy side of the tracks, believes attention to detail is the key to the President's success at the polls. "It's a kind of toughness," he says, "though not many people recognize it as that. He just works harder and longer than anyone else. When he got to L.A., it was all done. The others were only hoping." Actually the cultivated memory has always been a tool of American politicians. Reportedly George Washington could remember the name of anyone he had met once. As Adlai Stevenson said to James M. Farley at a national convention, "Hi, Jim. You know, I never forget a face." Honey Fitz, the East Boston boy who became mayor of all Boston, liked to talk about the "Irish Switch" — shaking hands with one voter while gossiping with a second — but Abraham Lincoln was practicing this technique a hundred years ago, following a precept which had been set forth in the Boston *Atlas* of 1836: "Those who would have votes must descend into the forum and take the voters by the hand."

What sets the mayor's grandson apart is his application of the principle. With him it has reached corporate proportions. Faces are not only remembered; every warm and willing body is enlisted as a volunteer. Operating under Larry O'Brien's First Law of Politics (the more campaigners, the better) Kennedy recruited two hundred and eighty-six secretaries and twenty-one thousand workers for one Massachusetts election. Long before his presidential nomination, lists of names were being broken down state by state, entered into card files, and coded. Intricate wall maps were also prepared, though the candidate never seemed to need any. He carried them in his mind. "When he launched the big primary drive in Hyannis Port he lectured us on the entire country," O'Brien says. "Some of the people there, even though they had worked with him before, were amazed at his knowledge of political nuances. He could discuss Cuyahoga County in Ohio then. He knew who the powers there were, who to see, what to say. He could do this coast-to-coast, and he did — for three hours."

The President is proud of his political skills. Although he vigorously denies it, one member of his staff has the impression that he received an ironic pleasure from Adenauer's loss in last year's election. "*Der Alte* had played the virtuoso," the aide observes, "insisting that he had an instinctive feeling for the Germanic character, and he stirred a little professional jealousy in our man." Our man didn't acquire his knowledge of the American character from his readings in history, from Harvard's Professor Holcombe, or from any of the political scientists around him. He won it, as he won elections, in the forum, where his memory was harnessed to his staying power. Kennedy's fidgeting hand has never been too tired for one more Switch. On the eve of his re-election to the Senate in 1958, with landslide victory over a Hobson's choice Republican already conceded to him, he was riding back to his headquarters in a stupor of exhaustion. Suddenly he spied a woman crossing the street. His hand was blooded — literally — with the ferocious amiability of campaigning, but he mumbled, "Stop the car," wobbled out, and gave her a final, tremulous, I'd-appreciate-your-vote hand-shake.

Today O'Brien keeps a different kind of card file, containing entries for every congressman. Each bears helpful notations: names of friends, relatives, lodge affiliations, etc. He uses this information effectively, and so does his employer, during coffee hours and meals with men from Capitol Hill. The President makes it a point to remember legislators' birthdays; sometimes he telephones them to gabble about the days when they were members of the same cheery club, and once he swooped down by helicopter to attend a luncheon on Harry Byrd's country estate. These aren't casual social gestures. He is courting them, as they, and he, court constituents. The first President since Andrew Johnson to have served in both House and Senate, Kennedy makes a wily suitor, and he doesn't rely entirely on his endearing young charms. Sometimes he tries logic, promoting his trade program by showing tariff charts to congressional guests. Other times O'Brien, his Cyrano, lets them peep at his popularity polls. Kennedy's hidden persuaders are highly diverse — he used Ayub Khan as a foreign aid lobbyist — and they include the knuckle-duster. When O'Brien isn't busy with Hill liaison he turns to patronage, a subject of vast interest at the other end of Pennsylvania Avenue.

In this game the President's great stake is his prestige. Any Chief Executive's prestige is in constant flux. It grows when he takes a stand and wins, shrinks when he loses, wastes away if he is inert. Wastage is unlikely in this Administration. Some people think Kennedy tries too hard, but that is his nature. He keeps looking for winning combinations — urging policy changes on the Federal Reserve Board, say, or directing Secretary Goldberg to referee labor negotiations — and to the exasperation of Ken O'Donnell, who arranges his appointments, he persists in receiving an astonishing number of individuals. "It's hard not to get invited to the White House these days," he remarked during his first year. Invitations are scarcer now, though many are still welcomed, including titans of the press. Kennedy confers regularly with Salinger, meets publishers, and is interviewed by such alien Krocks as Alex Adzhubei of *Izvestia.* "A lot of his visits are pure public relations," one of his professorial assistants concedes. "Let's face it," says O'Brien. "He sells himself."

His self-sell reduces the dangers of open ruptures

at home. National leaders everywhere crave unified support — Kennedy, perhaps, more than most. "Naturally," he says. "There is a desire to maintain basic agreement." Yet in a democracy attempts at a solid front can be hazardous. Joe Cannon claimed that McKinley kept his ear so close to the ground it was full of grasshoppers. "I can't talk to you now," says the premier in an old European story; "there go my followers." Faith that political guile can win major issues without a fight may lead to jeopardy of an entire program, and the President is being watched carefully in that light. James M. Burns, in his pre-election biography of Kennedy, suggested that he "might have difficulty" doing more than "responding to political pressures and gusts of opinion." Today Burns comments, "He said he would be a party President, and he's not. He said he wouldn't be above the battle, and he is." The President, says Gore Vidal, "is reluctant to spend any of his popularity." Vidal remembers telling Kennedy how difficult it was to cast Frank Lovejoy's part in *The Best Man*. The President asked why, and "I explained that actors don't like to play unpopular roles; they become actors because they want to be admired. He smiled and nodded at once. Most people would have trouble understanding, but he saw it immediately."

This may be figmental. Like all great politicians, Kennedy has a knack for putting himself in someone else's shoes. During the war he took a gunboat from Tulagi to Rendova on a routine run. Jim Reed was aboard; so was a green ensign. After they reached the base Reed remarked to the skipper that he had seen the new officer in his tent, crying. "Jack didn't say anything," Reed recalls, "but shortly after that I looked for him, and he was gone. I looked everywhere, for two and a half hours. Finally I found him. He'd been with that ensign all that time, talking to him, calming him down." Those who charge Kennedy with a lack of warmth have in mind his inability, or reluctance, to arouse ideological fervor; none doubt this instinctive tact, which recurs in his life with the persistence of a sonata theme. Burns tells how he asked for the President-Elect's vacant Senate seat. "I guess I'm about a hundred and fiftieth on the list," he said to him, "but I want to put my name in." "No, Jim, you're not a hundred and fiftieth," Kennedy replied. "As a matter of fact, you're fourth or fifth." "I was so elated at this promotion," Burns says with a grin, "that it was a week before I realized he'd said no." During a White House reception for Secretary Dillon the line got stuck, and the most junior guest found himself vis-à-vis the President; they talked for about five minutes, and as the line moved on the young man, who is in the Treasury, realized that they had spent the entire time discussing the problems of a young Treasury man. Learning in Paris that de Gaulle is distracted by visitors who smoke in his office, Kennedy quietly put his cigars away. And when he visited Rayburn's Dallas hospital, and the mother of a child in braces asked whether he would have time to talk to her son, he made the time. Next day a reporter asked the mother if she was a Republican. "I *was*," she replied.

Nevertheless it is true that the President is sustained by confidence in what one member of his Cabinet has called "the integrity of compromise." And somehow the phrase does lack razzle-dazzle. Although every politician is a compromiser, most attempt to dress the product attractively. The chief ribbon for the Kennedy package was picked up at a party before his acceptance of the 1960 nomination, when Walt Rostow, now Counsellor of the State Department, told the candidate, "I know what the first sentence of your speech ought to be. You ought to say, 'This country is ready to get moving again, and I'm prepared to lead it.'" Since the inaugural there have been periodic assurances of movement, but political shellbacks expect something more. They want an embattled chieftain, a Horatius; a leader who will give the world a kick in the old kazzazza.

Because they measure Kennedy by their yardsticks, they fail. He baffles them, and they blame him. Blaming the President is an American custom almost as old as bundling. He is, after all, the biggest target in the land, and the formation of every presidential cult is followed by the congealment of an anti-cult. "Remember," Woodrow Wilson warned his daughter when his first Administration was sailing along smoothly, "the pack is always waiting to tear one to pieces."

Andrew Jackson was portrayed as an adulterer, Lincoln as a baboon, Harry Truman as a haberdasher. Thomas Jefferson was "Mad Tom," and even Washington was scarred. "I am accused of being the enemy of America, and subject to the influence of a foreign country," he wrote Mad Tom, ". . . and every act of my Administration is tortured, in such exaggerated and indecent terms as could scarcely be applied to Nero, to a notorious defaulter, or even to a common pickpocket." That passage was once quoted by John Kennedy, who added: "But he stood firm." Kennedy's own posture is illumined by a glance at the devices which, enriched by the family treasury, won him the office. There isn't a firework in the lot. They were selected on the theory that the United States has changed as its face has changed, that fresh approaches are required in a country which is no longer a land of cracker barrels, front porches, woodsheds, or, until recently, of rocking chairs.

His methods are very like those of the Establishment — of the transferred Oxonian — and they were introduced in the most inauspicious of environments. He made his debut in the burlesque house of American politics. "We have a fine party," a Massachusetts Democrat once said. "The only trouble with it is that we have ten thousand leaders." He might have added that they all wore baggy pants. Anything went in Boston, provided it was vaudevillian. The ambassador can recall two lackeys telling his father, "Pat, we voted a hundred and twenty-eight times today," and

Ted Kennedy recounts the story of Honey Fitz going to a prize fight, climbing into the ring, and making a speech. "Everybody tried to stop him, and no one could. He went on for fifteen minutes, with fights breaking out all over the place. You can't imagine Jack doing that. Those days are dead."

They are also mourned. Ted's own entourage includes men who speak reverently of "the master," by whom they do not mean the President. They are thinking of fun-loving Jim Curley, the Purple Shamrock. Curley always left them laughing. He called Saltonstall "Pinocchio" and the crowd guffawed and stamped its feet, and old-timers treasure his comment on the appointment, to a minor post, of Endicott Peabody Saltonstall. "All three of them?" the Shamrock asked. In the postwar years such mummery still dominated Boston politics, and Jack Kennedy's ambitions were the target of a couple of choice custard pies. One buffoon passed the word that Kick Kennedy had married a descendant of Oliver Cromwell, that evil man; another predicted that thanks to Jack, the St. Lawrence Seaway would start "right at the front door of the Merchandise Mart in Chicago, which is owned by old Joe Kennedy."

This is a game any number can play. If old Joe's son had opted for slapstick, he could have engaged a troupe of stipendiary churls to spread the classic counter rumors — that his opponents had been excommunicated, jailed on morals charges, and endorsed by the Planned Parenthood Federation — or to pound on doors in the middle of the night, demanding that the enraged inhabitants vote for the opposition. There would have been plenty of volunteers. His name brought a mob of them to the Hotel Bellevue. "Kennedy was wonderful with those *Last Hurrah* characters," says Jim Reed. "He never promised them anything, but they all had the impression that something would be coming to them, because that was what they wanted to believe." "They crowded around him like moths around a flame," Billings remembers. "His two rooms were jam-packed every day from 6 A.M. on."

In the beginning the candidate welcomed everyone; he was glad to have any support at all. Then, slowly, he began separating the men from the boys — and keeping the boys. Kennedy's patrician vote-cadgers were making their bow. The aging mountebanks were sent out to the street, where they may still be found, chuckling over old Curley stories. Inside, Billings and Reed became typical members of what Kennedy called his "junior brain trust." Both were doing graduate work at Harvard, and that fitted: the junior trust was a potpourri of eager intellectuals, veterans, gray-flanneled ex-roommates, out-of-state Protestant Republicans, and one Harvard valet named Taylor. In Boston this was incredible; it was like enlisting the Houston Jaycees to mastermind a Bombay campaign against Krishna Menon. Honey Fitz tried to be helpful. He sent over some seasoned precinct workers, who stared at what one leathery pol called "all those crew-cut college boys in the silk suits" and boggled. This was politics? They departed for a quick belt in the Bellevue bar and left their old friend's grandson to his fate. It is highly improbable that any of them suspected what that fate would be.

The young man's first triumph seemed to be a freak. It could only be attributed to his father's money, and that continued to be the accepted explanation, even after he had won a third congressional term without spending a penny. He knew nothing about traditional political stagecraft, nor would he learn. No wakes for him, no paupers on the payroll; in office he retained his aversion to corn and went back to the same new drawing board. "The way to get along," Sam Rayburn told him, "is to go along." Kennedy wouldn't go along. As his father once said, "Nobody tells Jack what to do unless he wants to be told." The callow congressman refused to sign a pardon petition for Curley when that grand old man, through some misunderstanding, was imprisoned for fraud, and he continued to consult witless youths. Stalking his Senate seat, he chose as chief scout a lawyer who had played JV football with him at Harvard. If anything, the age of his advisers was growing more tender; Bobby's generation had left college now, and from it he recruited O'Donnell and Richard K. Donahue. By now Kennedy had become openly contemptuous of political hacks, while they, in turn, could only marvel that he had the effrontery to be a candidate for anything. His personal organization — it was entirely personal — was so ignorant that its members didn't know who the big wheels of the party were; at a national convention they snubbed Mayor Richard J. Daley of Chicago and Carmine De Sapio, who in those bygone days was a power to reckon with. Meanwhile Himself was seen reading John Buchan's biography of Cromwell and — worse and worse — Paul Blanshard's *American Freedom and Catholic Power*. Retribution, both divine and secular, seemed certain.

Powerful secular forces in his own party affixed him with the evil eye. Curley, out of stir, swore vengeance and was delighted when the chump volunteered to commit hara-kiri by running against Lodge, a task nobody else wanted. To make certain everything went ill for Kennedy, the Shamrock turned his coat and quietly slipped across the party line to help Lodge, who had defeated him in another Senate race sixteen years before. The returns came in: strike one against the bosses. Four years later the greenhorn tangled with John McCormack, the state's senior Democrat, and the scavengers waited to pick up the pieces. The result was strike two. Then, as the Eisenhower years waned, two of the mightiest figures in the national leadership — Rayburn and Truman — held a Washington tête-à-tête in the back seat of a Cadillac and decided that whoever the next President was, his name wouldn't be Kennedy. That was followed by strike three. Every Indian sign had failed. Jack had not only foiled the bullies; he had thrashed them soundly. Running for reelection to the Senate in

1958, he received approximately three of every four votes cast, the largest margin in the history of Massachusetts elections. After the McCormack joust the pieces the scavengers found were McCormack's; the tyro had officially replaced him as state leader. And in 1960, Rayburn and Truman never got off the ground.

Meanwhile his Republican opponents, one by one, were entering the shadow of eclipse. There are few signs that they will emerge soon. As President he has occupied stage center, and the G.O.P. has been obliged to move over. When the Republican National Committee met early in 1962, Chairman William Miller compared the President to Hitler and asked for funds to investigate the men around him. Kennedy didn't rise to the bait. He felt the charges were self-defeating, and some of Miller's colleagues seemed to agree. ("Who ever heard of Schlesinger back where I came from?" complained a man from the West. "We're in a vacuum at the moment," a comitteeman confessed.) Rockefeller excepted, the party's leadership sounds rather daunted, which may puzzle some, for Nixon came very close in 1960. But the gracile Democratic plurality that autumn had encouraged hopes of a G.O.P. dawn in 1961, and the dawn had proved false. Richard J. Hughes was supposed to lose the governorship of New Jersey by eighty thousand votes. All the polls said so. Then the President's road show, still shunning ballyhoo, entered the state and pulled Hughes across.

One upset is a freak. A string of them is a trend, and clearly this trend says something about the motion of the United States which is far more significant than Rostow's slogan. The country isn't ready to get moving again; it has been moving for some time, and its political locus is away from bossism, sectionalism, and partisanship. American mothers, Gallup found, often think of their sons as future Presidents; rarely as future politicians. The electorate doesn't fancy bowlers and smelly cigars. The new breed smokes less, and the voters enjoy it more. From his beginnings in Curley's old congressional district, Kennedy sensed that this was to be the era of what Leo Egan calls "the coffee-filled room." In Massachusetts shillelaghs had become vulgar. Catholics yearned for respectability, so the candidate carefully fostered the impression that he was an office-seeker of another stripe, reserved and unpretentious. "The young Irish had settled in places like Belmont, Winchester, Brookline, and Lexington," O'Brien says. "These are Republican towns, and they didn't want to be a minority, so they switched their registrations. Then in '52 the President broke through and they had a new leader. The significant thing about that vote was the breakdown. In the cities he ran abreast of the Democratic ticket, but outside the cities he ran way ahead of it. That's where he won."

Kennedy's shunning of kingmakers naturally made them uneasy, and his presidential behavior has justified their suspicions. In New York he supported the

rebel challenge to Tammany Hall; he even denounced the awarding of choice ambassadorships to
big party contributors, a blow which struck some venerable Democrats as being sharper than a serpent's
tooth. Yet it would be naïve to suppose that he is
prompted by idealism. No politician can afford to be
any better than he ought to be — until he retires —
and Kennedy isn't hostile to classic politics. His inno-
vations are technological. An age of wide screens demands mannerly candidates and open covenants. The
President has decided to accept television debates
with his 1964 opponent (and to demand similar debates for lesser offices) because his audience will accept nothing less. Connivance and evasiveness are
trademarks of the old pols; the new style is an inver-
sion of them. The people liked Ike because he seemed
above the ward scramble, and they like his successor
because, as he once said, he returned from the war
"not as a Democratic wheelhorse who came up from
the ranks — I came in sort of sideways."

He might have added that after slithering in, he
found himself right in the middle of the road. That
is where most Americans see themselves; their national purpose is to avoid the ruts on either side. The
President is farther down the road than they are. He
knows, as they do not, that big government is here to
stay, and he recognizes that the frustrations of co-
existence are permanent. Their lag accounts for the
gap between their regard for him and their disregard
for much of his program; it is hard for them to see the

implications of the Common Market, which may become the greatest issue of this Administration. But
they can see him and they trust him. Every Chief
Executive mirrors his time. When the Union was
riven, Lincoln was a figure of anguish. The nation
was boisterous sixty years ago; so was Theodore
Roosevelt. Coolidge slept a lot, and Eisenhower made
folks happy. Kennedy is bland, wary, polite. The
qualities he doesn't have are the qualities the young
marrieds in the suburban developments don't want.
He lacks emotional fire, and they distrust fire; they
associate oratory with hams. The message of his career is clear: the new strength is a muted strength.
The new leader must be restrained, and aloof from
alien corn.

The older generation seldom got that message. Between it and him lay a deep and often unbridgeable
chasm. Basic communication became difficult; in
1960 the junior brain trusters used older recruits —
men like John Bailey of Connecticut and Hyman
Raskin of Chicago — as interpreters. On the eve of
the election Dick Donahue watched a group of elder
Democrats who were eying the nominee enviously.
"You know," Donahue said to Theodore H. White,
"they can't understand this. They think he has a
trick. They're listening to him because they think if
they learn the trick they can be President, too." Today a White House aide believes that in the capital,
where so many men of power are the ambassador's
age, "this generational thing is more wrenching than

any bill, any issue, any program." Another aide, Larry O'Brien, observes that "Through the years he has been consistently underestimated by the pols. Back in '52 he surprised Lodge, and in '60 he astonished Johnson. They just can't get it."

Their children get it, though. All the talk of surging Goldwater youth is eyewash. Opinion samplers have observed that the younger the voters, the stronger their preference for Kennedy. If everyone over thirty had stayed away from the polls, he would have been swept into the White House. His peers have never underrated him. Indeed, some of them have anticipated him. In 1941 the Navy ordered him to lecture to some Charleston, South Carolina, factory workers on sabotage. Lem Billings, in town for his brother's wedding, went over to listen. "He didn't know much about the subject," Billings says, "but he'd done his homework, and he gave them a good, impressive speech about the two types of incinerator bombs. Then he made the mistake of asking for questions. The first one was, 'How do you tell the difference when they hit?' He didn't hesitate. He said, 'I'm glad you asked that question. Next week we'll have a specialist in that field give a demonstration.' Right then I picked him as a political comer." Later Billings found his political arguments so persuasive that he changed his own registration from Republican to Democratic. All the officers who were with Kennedy in PT's, says Jim Reed, "came back from the war talking about him, sold on him." Red Fay was more spe-

:ific; his San Francisco neighbors remember that he eturned from the Pacific predicting that a naval lieu- enant named Kennedy would be President some day. The following spring Red went East to help crush the :ongressional aspirations of the ex-WAC major and he Joseph Russos. Late in the summer of 1961 he was visiting his home, and while going through some old papers he found a note he had written home from the Bellevue, where he joined the roommate legion.

I am living here with Jack Kennedy, who is really out on a big scale, he had scribbled on April 5, 1946. *If by chance the West Coast papers carry a story about me running for Secretary of the Navy, kill it. It's the Undersecretary of the Navy I get.*

The scribbler's present address is the Pentagon. Three days after scaling the biggest hurdle of all, Jack Kennedy — who never saw this letter — ap- pointed his old shipmate Undersecretary of the Navy.

Undersecretary Fay's prescience startles him now, though it shouldn't. He had seen the future before. In the first week of August, 1943, he was executive officer of PT-167, and on Florida Island, off Gua- dalcanal, he encountered the commander of a second PT boat, who told him how a third had been rammed and sunk by a Jap destroyer.

"There was a tremendous explosion — then every- body was gone," said the eyewitness.

Red bluntly called him a liar. "I don't believe it," he said. "Not everybody. It couldn't happen."

At the time this was a minority report. The official

opinion was that the crew of the rammed craft had gone down in enemy waters, and that her skipper, Lieutenant (j.g.) John F. Kennedy, aged twenty-six, had been killed in action.

FOUR

Flat Out, All Out

ONE MONDAY MORNING in the late summer of 1961 a glittering 707 jet bearing the official seal of the President of the United States landed in Washington, and its chief passenger prepared to debark. Leaving his compartment amidships, he found two other men awaiting the ramp — a Secret Service man and a friend who, like John Kennedy, is a veteran of the Solomon Islands campaign.

The President turned to the Secret Service agent. "Man, do you realize you're standing next to one of of the great heroes of the last war?" he asked him gravely. His friend began to redden. The famous voice continued reverently: "Yes, in those years" (*yee-ahs*) "he put in more time on coral reefs, tied up more Japanese troops, won more victories single-handed against-all-odds with his back-against-the . . ."

By now the guest was scarlet, the agent grinning broadly. Both were aware that an authentic hero stood there, and that it wasn't either of them. John Kennedy's wartime valor has become as much a part of American lore as Theodore Roosevelt's ride up Kettle Hill. John Hersey described it at the time in a *New Yorker* dispatch. A U. S. Navy oil painting in the White House shows the Japanese destroyer *Amagiri* ramming Kennedy's PT-109 on the tar-black night of August 2, 1943. Jack Warner, who voted for Dick Nixon, contracted to film a big-budget production depicting the time the lieutenant — to be played by Cliff Robertson — put in on coral reefs after the crash. Robert J. Donovan has written a book about PT-109, and on Kolombangara Island Donovan found that for nearly twenty years the natives have been singing a folk song about "Captain" Kennedy's bravery in Blacklett Strait. The singers were gratified to learn that the captain had been picked headman of his tribe back home.

Actually he hadn't any business being in the islands twenty years ago. He wasn't fit. After he had been reported killed, a fellow officer wrote home, "The man that said the cream of a nation is lost in war can never be accused of making an overstatement of a very cruel fact"; but the headman-to-be certainly wasn't the physical cream. To many Americans today he seems the eternal youth — wiry and agile, with the profile of a Lindbergh and the glowing health of a Merriwell. This image is a triumph of will. His life has been dogged by illness. There have been interludes, of course. During the Los Angeles convention he could elude reporters by jumping a fence; he was once a Burning Tree member, and before the Ottawa tree-planting he liked to practice chip shots on the White House lawn. But disability has always returned in one form or another. Although his spine improved in the winter of 1961-1962, lusty exercise is out. His big executive chair is of corrective design, and to minimize strain he must constantly wear both his corset and corrective quarter-inch lift in his left heel.

No single calamity is responsible for his medical history. He has had a series of physical mishaps — so many, indeed, that some of his friends wonder whether he may be accident-prone. As boys he and his older brother collided on bikes; young Joe was unhurt, but Jack required twenty-eight stitches. Aged fourteen, he had to drop out of school for a convalescence, the first in a series of interruptions which were to check his formal education again and again. When Westbrook Pegler advised Nixon to demand that Kennedy "quit talking the lace-curtain geechee and speak Americanese if he knows the American language after his years of dear old London school," he wrote with characteristic Peglerian exorbitance. Jack didn't even spend one year, or even one term in the London School of Economics; jaundice forced him to withdraw. Three months after entering Princeton he had to quit again, bedridden. The following autumn he switched to Harvard. Playing football as a sophomore, he sprained his back. As war approached he tried to enlist. The Army wouldn't take him. There was that back, and he was thin as a shad. After building up his body he made the Navy — which then decided he would be more useful at a desk.

In an early letter listing sisterly complaints against him Jean Kennedy had written, "He had a temperature of 102° one night, too, and Miss Cahill couldn't make him mind." Jack never was very good at minding, especially when sick. Once, when ordered to the Harvard infirmary with grippe, he sneaked over to the pool an hour each day to practice his backstroke, hoping the coach would send him in there against Yale. Instead his grippe had worsened, and the coach had picked another backstroker named Richard Tregaskis. Afterward Tregaskis went out to the islands and wrote *Guadalcanal Diary*. Jack also reached Guadalcanal waters, because he wouldn't mind the Navy any better than he had Miss Cahill. Objecting to the home front, he enlisted the aid of one of the most determined men in the world, his father. Joe Kennedy put heat on what he called "the brass who had been on my London staff," and the fleet changed its mind.

In the Pacific the ambassador's son was assigned

to a series of makeshift bases, all of them dreadful holes. Americans had thought of the South Seas as an exotic land where lazy winds whispered in palm fronds, and Sadie Thompson seduced missionaries, and native girls dived for pearls in fitted sarongs, like Dorothy Lamour. The charms of the women had been badly oversold; they were closer to Big Daddy Lipscomb than Lamour. If possible, the terrain was even less attractive. On Bougainville, bulldozers vanished in spongy bottomless swamps, and at Cape Gloucester — where sixteen inches of rain fell in a single day — twenty-five Marines were killed by huge falling trees. Jungles crawled with snakes, crocodiles, headhunters. As an officer Kennedy was entitled to a houseboy, but that wasn't much comfort; his boy turned out to be a cannibal whose culinary triumphs had included a missionary.

This was the heyday of the great gripe, and Jack didn't suffer in silence. To his brother Bobby he wrote that at a physical examination "I coughed hollowly, rolled my eyes, croaked a couple of times, but all to no avail." He was also addicted to the wartime lament "I've been shafted" — which, since it came out of his Harvard euphonium as "shahfted," earned him the sobriquet "Shafty." Yet when he had a chance to return stateside, he declined, although his aching back had grown worse. The nightly combat missions didn't help it. His boat was about as long as the presidential cabin cruiser *Honey Fitz*, which is where the

comparison stops. The cabin cruiser has carpets, cur-
tains, armchairs, beds. Aboard 109 the skipper slept
on a plywood board.

Years later a Midwestern youth asked him how he
happened to become a war hero. "It was involuntary,"
he replied. "They sank my boat." The explanation
omits a lot. The ramming left eleven seamen (the
seating capacity of *Honey Fitz* today) floundering in
seas that were shark-infested and swarming with
Japanese. One survivor was badly burned, and the
impact of the enemy destroyer had dealt Jack's
sprained spine a cruel blow; as he ricocheted against
his cockpit he had thought, "This is how it feels to be
killed." Nevertheless it was he who towed the injured
sailor for four hours, using the man's life jacket strap
as a towrope and leading the crew to an island over
three miles away. Because the strap was in his teeth
he swallowed a great deal of brine; he threw up on
the beach. His condition notwithstanding, next evening he breaststroked into the middle of the strait
with a .38 pistol and a battle lantern and treaded
water through the night, hoping to attract the attention of friendly craft. There were none.

Kennedys are strong swimmers — as a boy the
President could freestyle fifty yards in thirty seconds;
Caroline learned to swim in the summer of 1961, at
the age of three — but when the hot sun rose the
next morning he had been in the water for the better
part of a day and a half. The return to the island took
him five hours; he barely made it. Again he retched on

the shore, again he resolved to go on. Once more haul-
ing the helpless casualty, who survived the war to
become a California postman, he moved his men to a
second island, and then went on to a third with Ensign Barney Ross. Encountering friendly Melanesians,
he chiseled a message on a fragment of a coconut:
*Native knows posit he can pilot 11 alive need small
boat Kennedy.* The crude appeal reached an Australian coastwatcher named Arthur Reginald Evans.
Seven natives hid Jack under palm fronds in the bottom of a dugout and paddled him to Evans, after
which the coastwatcher's radio brought three liberat-
ing PT's from Rendova, thirty miles away.

To the rescuers the rescue seemed miraculous.
Two sister PT's had seen the crash, and it was assumed that all hands had been lost. Searches had
been perfunctory; the lost men had been mourned.
Not all their relatives were aware of it, however. On
Cape Cod, half a world away, eleven-year-old Ted
Kennedy was buying newspapers for his grandfather.
He glanced at the Boston *Herald* and jumped — four
drawings on the front page depicted the ramming
and the crew's deliverance. "I was dumfounded," he
says. "I hadn't been told anything about it." Only
one person on the Cape had known, and he hadn't
talked. Joe Kennedy had been informed that his son
was gone. He had lived with that report for four days,
saying nothing. Eighteen years later he could still remember coming in from his Hyannis Port stables and
seeing his wife rushing toward him. "I just turned on a

news broadcast," she was crying. "They say Jack's been saved. Saved from what?" The ambassador turned away. "Oh —" He shrugged deeply. "Nothing. It was nothing."

Since his first week as President the coconut fragment, encased in plastic, has been a fixture on John Kennedy's desk. His ordeal didn't diminish his love of the sea, acquired on the Cape as a child. Among his White House trophies are maps of the Solomons, the harpoon section of a dart gun, a well-thumbed copy of *Fishing Boats of the World,* and, mounted on the wall of a waiting room across from Ken O'Donnell's office, a huge sailfish he caught on September 16, 1953, while honeymooning at Acapulco, Mexico. As a bachelor congressman he sailed in Washington's tidal basin with Ted Reardon. Jacqueline Bouvier was courted aboard his twenty-four-foot sailboat off Hyannis Port, and when the sea is right he likes to take off for hour-and-a-half cruises aboard *Honey Fitz* or *Marlin,* his fifty-two-foot motor cruiser, reading newspapers in the stern or watching the First Lady zoom by on water skis. Mention the island war and his eyes light up, although, curiously, it wasn't until after his inaugural that he learned his chief benefactor's identity. The coastwatcher had been the object of a search far more elaborate than that for 109's castaways. It ended when Evans, now a Sydney accountant, called an Australian newspaper. He was invited to Washington, where the President apologized for forgetting to return his Japanese rifle eighteen years before.

In that setting the reunion struck a mellow note. The marooning, in the words of a wartime hit tune, was long ago and far away. There seemed to be no connection between then and now. Yet the lieutenant of those distant days was very like the President of today. He has matured, of course. A 1945 photograph shows him being decorated for heroism by Captain Frederick L. Conklin, USN. In it the reserve lieutenant looks as unstarched as a beer jacket. The Commander in Chief of the 1960's is suaver. Nevertheless, during a similar ceremony he did drop Alan B. Shepard's medal, and despite his awesome office he suggests the mobility and unorthodoxy of youth. "You know, I still find it hard to believe that fellow is President of the United States," says a veteran Washington correspondent, shaking his head. People Kennedy's age often share this attitude. "For some reason, Mr. President, your living in the same house with Lincoln's bed impresses the hell out of me," one of his former roommates told him. Sometimes he himself appears to feel that way, and defers to older men when all men, regardless of age, should defer to him. After leading John Diefenbaker to a battery of television cameras outside the White House he told him, "Now you make your statement while I go back to the office and get your coat."

As a young man he was exceptionally boyish. When Red Fay reported to a PT training center at Melville, Rhode Island, in 1942, he found a group of men playing touch. Among them was a stripling who, he thought, was "a high school kid horning in on the game." Next day he learned the urchin was Jack Kennedy, his instructor. After his rescue of 109's crew the skipper was ordered to brief a new batch of sailors on the Solomons. Meeting them on Tulagi, he told them to stand around him in a wide circle. But they couldn't take this beanpole with bars seriously. The instant he started talking the boots crowded in, yammering questions until he gave up and said if there was ever anything he could do for them, just let him know. ("The worst mistake I ever made. They've been letting me know ever since.") Later, during his first years in the capital, he was joined by the Kennedy family cook, who tried to put some flesh on him. She failed; he became weedier and weedier, reminding some colleagues of Jimmy Stewart playing *Mr. Smith Goes to Washington*. Jack's habits didn't help. His brush-cut carelessly combed with a little Wildroot, he would slip into a sweatshirt, pick up a baseball glove or a football, and sally out looking for a game. One November day in 1949 his Melville comedy with Fay was reenacted. Representative Kennedy was watching a squad of real high school kids practicing. He borrowed a uniform and joined them, and none of the players noticed anything unusual. The coach asked one, "How's the congressman doing?" "Is that what they call him?" asked the boy. "He needs a lot of work, Coach. What year's he in?"

On the Hill a seasoned lobbyist continually addressed him as "laddie." Tourists mistook him for a college student with a patronage appointment, and one morning in an elevator a stranger murmured to him, "Fourth floor, please." These awkward incidents persisted during his first days in the Senate. According to a page boy, the new member of the upper house was waved away from a special phone. "Sorry, mister," a guard told him. "These are reserved for the senators." And when he tried to board a presidential train in Springfield, Massachusetts, he was thrown off by James J. Rowley — who is now chief of his Secret Service. The ejected young pol wasn't offended, though there were times when he thought he and the congressional page boys should swap jobs, he wryly confessed to the Washington *Times-Herald*'s Miss Bouvier.

The President tells these stories about himself. His wit is cool, merciless, and surprisingly impartial. Of course, he enjoys taunting adversaries most. To a group of businessmen he said, "It would be premature to ask your support in the next election, and inaccurate to thank you for it in the past," and on another occasion he compared his election to a Notre Dame-Syracuse football game which had been won with a disputed penalty, adding that "I'm like Notre Dame. We just take it as it comes along. We're not giving it back." But neither allies nor relatives are exempt. If

one is maladroit, heavy on his feet, or just heavy —
Salinger has a tendency toward what posture charts
call stocky — he is not allowed to forget it. A friend,
comparing their common backgrounds, suggested
that he and the President were pretty much alike.
Kennedy peered at him a moment. "You're not at all
like me," he said. "You walk like a duck." A lawyer
wrote him that his racket-busting brother would make
a better Chief Executive. He replied, "I have consulted Bobby about it, and, to my dismay, the idea
appeals to him." When Bobby hesitated to enter the
Cabinet, the President-Elect reassured him that "We'll
announce it in a whisper at midnight so no one will
notice it." Critics, noticing it and disapproving of it,
protested that the future Attorney General had never
tried a case in court. "I can't see that it's wrong to give
him a little legal experience before he goes out to
practice law," John Kennedy told Washington's Al-
falfa Club. Afterward the appointee came up and
told him that he didn't think that was very funny.
His older brother commented that he would have to
kid himself; people liked it. Nobody can handle a
Kennedy like a Kennedy. "Yes, but you weren't kidding yourself," Bobby pointed out. "You were kidding
me."

Like Lincoln, the President is a mild practical
joker — before his voice became renowned he liked
to call people up and pretend he was someone else —
with an instinctive gift for drollery. During a discussion of office-seekers with a Southerner, he came to

he name of another Southerner. The man had applied for the governorship of the Virgin Islands. "That
ob usually goes to a Negro," he pointed out, "and he
sn't a Negro." He paused. "Is he?" It was the President who first said of Ted Kennedy's senatorial primary race against Eddie McCormack, the Speaker's
nephew, that "We'd rather be Ted than Ed." That was
during his 1962 Gridiron Club speech, when he also
remarked, "I know my Republican friends were glad
to see my wife feeding an elephant in India. She gave
him sugar and nuts. But of course the elephant wasn't
satisfied." The same evening he plunged a long
needle into both Arthur Krock and the capital's all-
white Metropolitan Club — "Krock criticized me for
not letting President Tshombe of Katanga come here,
so I told him we would work out a deal. I'll give
Tshombe a visa and Arthur can give him a dinner at
the Metropolitan Club."

Fred Holborn of the White House staff thinks the
Presidency has improved Kennedy's wit: "It used to
be rehearsed. Now it's sharper, more spontaneous,
less derivative. And ceremonies bring it out at its
best, because he likes to poke fun at rituals." Unable
to attend a testimonial luncheon for the Postmaster
General, the President sent a graceful apology and
added the postscript, "I am sending this message by
wire, since I want to be certain that this message
reaches you in the right place and at the right time."
In Wisconsin he was made honorary chieftain of an
Indian tribe. Donning his headdress he said, "Next

time I go to the movies to see cowboys and Indians, I'll be with us." Paying tribute to Clark Clifford for his services during the transitional period between the election and the inauguration, he announced that Clifford hadn't requested any reward — "all he asked in return was that we advertise his firm on the backs of the one-dollar bills."

His eye for the ridiculous also sharpens during crises. As the returns seesawed on election night 1960, he received a long distance call from Lyndon Johnson in Texas. His anxious staff awaited his version of the vice-presidential nominee's words. It was: " 'I hear *you*'re losing Ohio, but *we*'re doing fine in Pennsylvania.' " At the climax of the Cuban misadventure, Kennedy bipartisanship was embarrassed when Stewart Udall appeared on an ABC panel show and attributed the landing to Eisenhower planners. Afterward he was summoned to a phone. The White House was calling. Reportedly the President's first words were, "Which of us does not make mistakes?" The trouble with the status quo in Berlin, Kennedy has complained, is that there is too much quo and not enough status. And at the crucial moment of his Solomons feat — his deliverance from starvation — he was in top form. PT-157 raced in to meet him, recognition shots were exchanged, and a voice called, "Hey, Jack!" "Where the hell have you been?" he answered. "We've got some food for you," he was told. "No thanks," said Shafty. "I just had a coconut."

Those who assume that banter means indifference should reflect on his circumstances that night. He was emaciated, exhausted, and lacerated by coral wounds. If he had lacked pluck there would have been no rendezvous with PT-157. "The big thing that came out in Kennedy that week was his drive," Barney Ross says. "I knew it was useless for him to swim out in the water that first night. You couldn't stop him, though. He didn't make a federal case out of it, but there it was. He just had to find a way back. And then, when we were picked up, he couldn't wait to get another boat. Everything was go, go, go with him. If it had been up to the rest of us, we would've been content to sit there and wait to be rescued." Unaware that they had been written off, the crew thought Navy PBY's must be scouting the area, and with enemy troops all around — a barge of Japs passed within a few hundred yards of their first beach — Kennedy's island-hopping seemed an invitation to trouble. Eventually they realized that his go, go, go had saved them. Abandoned in hostile waters, he had driven himself as though the destiny of the United States were his personal responsibility. Today it is: and there is a connection.

The most humdrum wartime chore was a big one for him. "Very willing and conscientious," the Navy described him in his first promotion report, and he never gave cause for retraction. In training an ensign missed the boat one day, and the laggard has a vivid recollection of how "the future President gave me the worst chewing out of my life — demanding to know where I'd been, asking me where the country would be if everybody in the Navy doped off that way, practically telling me I'd lost the war." On routine cruise in the Solomons Kennedy kept telling his crew, "Let's get more speed." The hull couldn't move fast enough for him. He couldn't bear the thought that 171, say, or 162 might outrev 109. Once he decided to beat another boat home at all costs. There was a rule about running down docks, but Jack the nimble — still no minding — took a chance his engines would reverse, lost the chance, and shahfted the pier. He had to be first. That was his style, that is his style. Through the years the same note of urgency has recurred. On his way to nominate Stevenson in 1956 he kept clenching his right fist and whispering to himself, "Go!" Campaigning in the 1960 West Virginia primary, he would snap his fingers at red lights, muttering, "Let's go." After Nixon's concession that fall his first words were, "All right, let's go," and when the First Lady publicly embraced the President after a trip abroad he blushed and then growled at his chauffeur, "Let's *go!*"

Each time he was going somewhere different. The important thing was to get there, to have a goal and reach it. There has been hardly a moment when he wasn't drawing a bead on a target — on Yale, or Tojo, on a domestic or foreign competitor. An exception was the morning of November 9, 1960. He was probably President-Elect, but it wasn't official. After breakfast he took a stroll along the Cape Cod beach, and to Ted, who walked with him, he remarked that for a few days there would be nothing to do, no decisions to make — no place, in short, to go. Taking a break was an odd experience for him. His sense of purpose dates back to his childhood, when he named his first sailboat *Victura*, explaining vaguely that it meant "something about winning." In prep school he was voted most likely to succeed, not because Joe Kennedy was rich — that cut no ice at Choate — and certainly not for his dead C scholarship, which, as his father has pointed out, probably wouldn't admit him to Harvard today. He was most likely because he was most eager; because, in Joe's words, "He's always been a fighter." Unable to win a letter in anything, Jack was nevertheless active in hockey, baseball, and football. "He was much too light for the big teams," his Choate roommate remembers, "yet he was always out there." Kennedy's own verdict on those featherweight years gives some inkling of their stubborn sweat: "I wasn't a terribly good athlete, but I participated."

His love of participation for its own sake has been noted even by those who aren't convinced that he is a terribly good President. "He did everything around here today but shinny up the Washington Monument," James Reston wrote from Washington in the late winter of 1962, "and it was obviously too cold and icy for that." If something is happening, Kennedy wants it to happen to him: "I can't hold back the stops. I have to go flat out, all out." In the 1950's one of his friends was working for the Emerson Drug Company in Baltimore. The company wanted to give its executives a speed reading course, but was two short of the number needed for a special class. The friend called Washington, and the quorum was filled by Jack and Bobby, who also likes to be in on things. "The fact that one was a United States Senator and the other was busy with the McClellan Committee didn't matter," the friend says. "They couldn't pass up a chance for self-improvement." The Kennedys commuted regularly from Washington, and Jack was not only active; this time he won his letter, with twelve hundred words a minute.

For him the Baltimore course was a natural. It was emulous, it was cerebral and, most important, it increased his velocity. As Ross noted, the word for him is Go. In the White House his appurtenances include the two cabin cruisers, a helicopter, a fleet of high-powered automobiles, and four private jets, all of which he uses. From his first days as a freshman congressman he was known as "the young man in a hurry." If there wasn't an office available, he campaigned just the same, driving through the night to address lodge meetings and subsisting on cheeseburgers and malted milk. Representative Kennedy was stumping western Massachusetts three years before he stood for the Senate; Senator Kennedy was barnstorming the nation three years before his election to the Presidency, and to hie him forth he acquired his forty-passenger Convair — the new *Victura*. Although he admired Jacqueline Bouvier the first time he met her, there was a period of six months in their courtship when he didn't even have time to see her. Now and then he would call her from some pay phone, "with," as she has put it, "a great clinking of coins," but there were no love letters, unless you count the postcard she showed their wedding party. It was the only message she had ever received from her intended, and the total text read, *Wish you were here. Jack.* Friends have observed that after Caroline identified her mother, the first words she learned — "Daddy," "airplane," "car," "shoe," "hat," and "thank you" — included at least three denoting motion. The senator's vim fascinated and bemused his bride. Playing Monopoly in Hyannis Port, she sometimes grew drowsy and deliberately blundered to get the thing over with. "Does Jack mind?" she was asked. She smiled. "Not if I'm on the other side."

He tired of Monopoly, as he later tired of bridge, Chinese checkers, backgammon, and The Game. They weren't getting him anywhere, and he can't bear to waste time. The President, a friend says, "thinks of words as the shortest distance between two points." A man who puts things in a nutshell wins his respect. A rambler loses. In private Kennedy will talk for hours, "but only," as a Harvard adviser puts it, "if there is real Ping-pong in the conversation." One Administration appointee brought a big reputation to Washington. He had intellect, insight, and experience, yet his stock kept falling because he lacked concision. He talked on and on until he found himself transferred to a new job, with the White House out of earshot.

Kennedy doesn't like to be held up by a windbag, a red light, or, for that matter, by his own body. Life among the Melanesian savages didn't reduce his impatience with his own infirmities. It merely made him frailer — and more intolerant of his frailty. In Blacklett Strait the disc between his fifth vertebra and his sacrum was ruptured. Navy surgeons had patched up his back with a metal plate, but the hole over it didn't close. V-J Day found him no better. When the lights went on again all over the world he was hollow-cheeked, sciatic, malarial, and Atabrine-yellow, and his weight had fallen to one hundred and twenty-five pounds. He wasn't really in shape for sailing, let alone a political scrimmage. So he entered, and won, that first wide-open congressional race.

Despite hot baths, couches, and rocking chairs, his spine grew worse, and at his wedding there was real doubt over whether he would be able to kneel at the altar. He knelt. Somehow he was always able to make that extra effort, suppress the pain, and carry things off. In his senatorial campaign against Lodge he was feverish, scarcely able to move without crutches. Not many voters knew it, because when the time came to enter a hall he would thrust his props aside and manage without them — "how," a friend who was with him later remarked, "I'll never know." Jim Reed was then living in Longmeadow, Springfield's blue-chip suburb, and they would meet on Kennedy's western swings. Reed remembers that "he'd stand through endless receptions, and give a speech afterward, and after the speech we'd have a bull session in Springfield till midnight, and *then* he'd drive back to the Cape. I couldn't have done it — and I didn't have a bad back." Yet this couldn't go on forever. Something had to give, the senator or his health. Two years later physicians gave him a choice: either invalidism or spinal fusion surgery with, at best, a narrow chance of survival. He punched his crutches. "I'd rather die than spend my life on these things," he said. He received the last rites, went through two operations, hovered on the dark edge, and then recovered at his father's Palm Beach house.

Jack the quick couldn't just lie there. He had to climb back on the ball somehow. During an earlier illness he had taken advantage of the occasion by quizzing the staff about medical aspects of legislation — "a doctor told me F.D.R. shouldn't have run for that fourth term," he recalls, explaining his vote for the constitutional amendment which limits his own White House tenure to eight years. In Florida his throbbing vertebrae wouldn't permit him to doze for more than an hour or so. He tried painting landscapes, but that wasn't really getting him anywhere, so he began using the sleepless nights to improve his mind. Sometimes he studied. A PT shipmate who visited him during his convalescence remembers that he would read two hours at a time, making notes on a clipboard and spending fifteen or twenty minutes at the end of a session memorizing what he had written. "I saw him again two or three months later," the shipmate says, "and I asked him about some of those notes. They came out in a torrent." Other times the patient used his clipboard as a crude desk. Arthur Krock, another bedside visitor, watched him, "strapped to a board, with another board on top of him, writing *Profiles in Courage.*" Most sick men would have been content to wait — as 109's crew had wanted to wait — for external forces to deliver them. Few would have attempted to produce a book, and fewer would have brought it off. Pulitzer judges notwithstanding, *Profiles* is not brilliant history. The really singular thing about the book is that it was written at all.

Not everyone finds Kennedy's grit engaging. Some think it relentless, inhuman. His ambition is so very naked; they wish he'd camouflage it a little. After he picked his 1960 running mate he was asked by Adlai Stevenson, whose intentions are not nearly as conspicuous, why he had chosen Johnson. The candidate laid it on the line in five crisp words: "Because I want to win." To win he will go any distance. During a campaign telethon a rural woman called and asked him to do something about her roads. A travesty of diction followed. Kennedy couldn't understand her; he thought she was saying "rugs." "I really don't know what the President of the United States could do

about your rugs," he said in exasperation. After the
program, when someone solved her dialect, he
wanted to call back and explain. It was a small stake,
one vote, but the small stakes added up. In Reston's
opinion, "The man is a calculating machine, with
springs. He seems wound up and full of controlled
nervous energy."

Early in his Administration Kennedy remarked that
he had only four years in which to make good — an
odd observation, and a revealing one. He is fighting
the clock as well as the Russians, which explains his
long hours, his gibes at pomp, and his repeated mur-
muring, at pointless functions, "Let me out of here."
Once he feels he has extracted the last measure from
a White House interview, he swings out of his rocking
chair and lands on his feet. It is an effective gesture.
The President is standing, so his visitor must stand,
too, and one senses that the motion, in itself, gives
him a sense of exhilaration. His wardrobe reflects this
passion for activity. In cut and color it is appropriate
for a chief of state, but in weight it is almost collegiate.
Kennedy rejects apparel which would slow him down.
He has few vests or hats, only one topcoat, and no
overcoat at all. "The President," his tailor explains,
"has steam heat instead of blood."

At year's end, as the Chief Executive darted about
wintry Washington in light kit — there were just
three years left to make good now — an elderly patient lay in room 355 of Palm Beach's St. Mary's Hos-

pital, not far from the home in which *Profiles in Courage* was conceived. Richard Cardinal Cushing called and told him he would get well. The ambassador's stroke had affected his speech, but he made himself reply, "I . . . know . . . I . . . will." It was a promise. Within a month he was walking, reading, and watching television, and by April he could greet the President at the airport. The swiftness of that partial recovery shows that John Kennedy hasn't the only strong constitution in the country. Indeed, there is a clear relationship between the older man's vigor and his son's. Because Joe had spirit, he raised a spirited family. "Everything begins in childhood," he said in 1961. "If a boy runs off to play in a jazz band" — his expression revealed how horrible an example he thought that was — "there's something in that family that's wrong, and it goes way back." Way back in the early 1930's he was goading his sons. If young Joe and Jack lost a sailboat race, his rage was a caution; the only way to avoid it was to win. And victory was tangible, it was secular. In many large Catholic families a son goes into the priesthood and a daughter becomes a nun. Bobby and one of his sisters considered devoting their lives to their religion, but their father was intent on things of this world. "Joe had a dynastic impulse," according to Arthur Krock. "He had to be the first Irish ambassador to Britain. He had to have a son become President of the United States. And, by God, he did it."

There can be little doubt that he meant to do it. In

the opening pages of *I'm for Roosevelt* he declared that "I have no political ambitions for myself or my children." The disclaimer is hard to credit. Questioned about it after his son's inauguration, he offered a curious annotation: "I wasn't thinking of the Presidency then. I just wanted them to be useful civic servants. If they'd become sheriffs or selectmen, that would've been O.K. with me." Sequiturwise, this was non. The idea of a Kennedy even starting on so low a level is preposterous. Nor could Joe have settled for that. Clearly he was a father of great expectations; Jack's schools were hardly those of an apprentice bailiff. The 1959 Gridiron Club show probably came closer to the truth when a character playing the ambassador sang:

> *All of us, why not take all of us?*
> *Fabulous — you can't live without us*
> *My son Jack heads the procession*
> *Then comes Bob, groomed for succession. . . .*

Since the procession reached the Executive Mansion, repeating jokes about it has become a national pastime. One wit predicted that "We'll have Jack for eight years, Bobby for eight, and Teddy for eight. Then it'll be 1984." In an apocryphal story the President pins a medal on John Glenn and says, "You're doing pretty well for someone who isn't in the family." Joe's proprietary attitude has encouraged this sort of thing; so many of his comments about the Ken-

nedys have been laced with *I-my-me*. Of Ted's im-
pending Senate candidacy he said, "We aren't ready
to announce that yet," and he confided to this writer
that he found the President's first State of the Union
address evocative of *I'm for Roosevelt*, though a
comparison of the two texts was unrewarding. Later
that day, strolling across Manhattan, he declared,
"Bobby's the best Attorney General since Stone," and
then paused, nodding significantly. Only later did his
visitor recall that Attorney General Harlan Fiske
Stone went on to become Chief Justice of the Supreme Court, and that conceivably the ambassador
may have envisaged family leadership in all three
branches of the government. Asked whether this was
farfetched, an acquaintance of the Kennedys' said
slowly, "I don't know. He *is* greedy."

Joe has never thought of himself as greedy. His attitude has been that America made him rich, and
that he has been repaying the debt by contributing
his children's gifts to the country. The ambassador-to-
be began instilling a Samaritan sense in the civic-
servants-to-be while they were babes and he was still
battling in the market place. Money wasn't considered a fit topic for familial dinner conversations.
"Big businessmen are the most overrated men in the
country," he told them. "Here I am, a boy from East
Boston, and *I* took 'em. So don't be impressed." Instead they argued about current events. "I raised
them to be active in public service," he said proudly
when the procession was fanning out across Wash-

ington, "and every one of them is. Every one of my sons-in-law, too. All except Peter Lawford." (Mr. Lawford, who married the President's sister Pat, is an actor.)

Lem Billings has vivid childhood memories of the Kennedy's family table. "It wasn't like any other dinner table," he recalls. The children had to be in their places five minutes early, and "the father kept the conversation on a high level. If you didn't talk about world affairs, you just didn't talk." Billings's conclusions would have surprised the ambassador, however. "Joe Kennedy likes to project a hardheaded image," he says. "Actually he's one of the most emotional people I've ever known. I think he didn't want his love for his children to overwhelm them, and talking about impersonal matters was one way to avoid it." Whatever the reason — dynastic impulse, patriotism, a surfeit of affection — a gauntlet was flung on the table, and each child lunged for it. Jack Kennedy's youthful devotion to the New York *Times* was one answer to the challenge. Virtually all of them became highly articulate in their teens; young Joe argued confidently with Harold Laski, and Kick Kennedy could logomachize with Winston Churchill. An exception was Bobby. His youth kept him seated down among the girls, outclassed, subdued. But little brother was down there watching, and in manhood, after a score of public speaking courses and countless evenings in front of mirrors, he untied his tongue. Bobby paid a price for this unleashing. In a glib family his delivery seems harsh, almost metallic. Teddy didn't face the forensic obstacle, because when he reached adolescence the big debaters had graduated. "By the time I was old enough to join in, there wasn't even a ban on talking business at the table," he says. "It wasn't necessary any more. These other things just seemed more important." Ted had another problem, though. As a Harvard freshman he found himself falling behind the standards set there by his three brothers, so he cheated. His subsequent suspension caused, as he delicately calls it, paternal "unhappiness." Two years later Ted entered Harvard again, and this time he went the distance. Joe's family script had made no provision for failure.

The ardor with which the Kennedys followed their father's lead has impressed even him. On the eve of his illness, before son-in-law Stephen Smith left the State Department to handle family affairs in New York, he wondered aloud whether he had gone too far. "I wish I'd saved *one* boy for the business," he said. "Here I am, seventy-three and I could drop dead any minute, and I have to keep working because they're in these other things." At the same time, he speculated about the parental role in shaping children. Perhaps, he reflected, it had been exaggerated. Barring business absences, he had been as attentive as a father could be, and certainly his wife was a devoted mother. Yet he wasn't at all certain that was the explanation: "Don't ask me what we did to make them this way. I don't know. Sure, I could give you some pat answers, but I've thought about it a lot, and I can't think of a single thing we tried that some of my friends haven't tried with very different results. If I knew what it was, I'd bottle it and sell it." He kept returning to one notion, though. "Competition — that's what makes them go. They're all competitive, including the girls. In fact, Eunice has more drive than Jack or even Bobby."

His daughter Eunice is the wife of R. Sargent Shriver, director of the Peace Corps. One Saturday she, Jean Smith, and Ethel Kennedy stopped by the White House for a swim in the pool. Afterward they decided to poke around the residential apartment, looking at new paintings. They thought the first family was in Virginia, so they went through the bedrooms, too, and in the last of them they discovered (and awakened) the President of the United States. The visitors can't be blamed. Presidents must nap, but it's something new for this calisthenic family. The Kennedys are what is known as vigorous stock. They will compete with anybody, in any field. Some of the in-laws have just as much moxie as the charter members — when Ethel picked up Marian Anderson for a concert, she entertained her by singing to her in the car — and the sisters, like their brothers, are fierce contenders in the tribal gymkhanas of touch, tag, and kick-the-can. Sex is not recognized as a handicap, nor is age. No holds are barred for women and children; everybody plays for keeps. Jacqueline made a ladylike retirement from lawn sport only after she had hurt an ankle, and Red Fay, returning to the Pentagon after a joy-through-strength weekend on the Cape, said grimly, "Of course, I know what they were really trying to do. They were trying to kill the old redhead." Hyannis Port games can be rougher than anything, including McCarthyism. The late Senator McCarthy wasn't even in their softball league. Once when he was visiting the ambassador they tried him at shortstop and then benched him. He had made four errors.

Fratricidal touch, as the world knows, is their specialty. They even have family-league touch trophies. There always seems to be an inflated football around somewhere — the day the country voted their top player into the White House he was flipping one around with Bobby and Teddy. As Harvard freshmen all the boys played end, a position requiring stout hearts. Jacqueline excepted, all hale members of the family are either passers or pass receivers today. John Kennedy and John Unitas are probably the two most famous quarterbacks in the country, and Kennedy, like Unitas, has thrown the long gainer on many memorable occasions, including Pearl Harbor Day. One published account has it that he spent the afternoon of December 7, 1941, in Griffith Stadium, watching the Redskins upend the Philadelphia Eagles, but according to Billings, who was with him, they were playing touch. Donning old clothes, they had driven downtown looking for a pickup game. After a fierce scrimmage with strangers around the Washington Monument, they headed home and heard the Pearl

Harbor bulletin on the car radio. Kennedy's first re-action was "to get into something." Though he was al-ready in naval intelligence, that didn't count. It was too much like being a spectator, he said. He might not make a terribly good combat officer, but he still wanted to participate.

The day of his wedding photographers were agog to see deep scratches on his face. It wasn't anything serious. He had merely toppled out of bounds and into a bed of roses the day before. Secret Servicemen were similarly startled when the new President-Elect celebrated his election by joining an internecine fam-ily fray, calling signals for one squad while Bobby (who won) led the other. In the months that followed John Kennedy kept this up, and nobody knew quite so well how to frighten Dr. Travell. Since then she has sidelined him, but he was a great star. Playing golf one day he learned that the country club's as-sistant pro had been a gridiron flash. Fishing the ubiquitous football from a car trunk, he offered to take him on. The pro teamed up with a rangy caddie, Kennedy with a friend. The first side with three touchdowns was to be the winner. "He threw three perfect strikes to me," says the friend, who spent most of his time in the makeshift end zone. "That gives you some idea what kind of a touch football player the President is. What's more, I dropped one, so he pitched me a fourth." The final score was J.F.K., 18; Pro, 0.

Woodrow Wilson, brooding over the strains of office, reflected that future generations would be obliged to pick their Presidents from the ranks of "wise and prudent athletes." Several athletes had preceded him; Teddy Roosevelt wasn't himself unless he'd had a brisk workout, and John Adams liked his swims in the buff. President Kennedy, however, has recruited a whole string of athletes. Sorensen's adoption of Kennedyisms includes a fondness for touch; McNamara plays squash Saturdays; Udall climbs mountains and, now and then, trespasses on private property and gets bawled out. Edward R. Murrow, who detests the strenuous life himself, calls it the "new zeal" Administration. It is a better team, in the literal sense, than anything Eisenhower could have put into the field. Among the inaugural starters were Udall (Arizona basketball ace), Secretary of Agriculture Orville Freeman (Minnesota varsity quarterback), Ken O'Donnell (Harvard football captain), former Deputy Attorney General — now Associate Justice — Byron "Whizzer" White (Colorado All-American), and, of course, the Attorney General, who played for the Cantabs and still keeps in shape despite the outrage of Jimmy Hoffa, who protested that Bobby's sporty manner of dress was undignified and was ruining this country's reputation abroad.

The President himself, though sedentary now, isn't quiescent. His key is still C major. In his own restless way he is exercising all the time. A reporter observed that he "never sits in a chair; he bivouacs in it." Two White House chairs have collapsed under the stress.

Once he capsized a swivel job — dumping himself on the floor — and on another occasion an antique blew up under him. It happened spectacularly, in the middle of a conference with congressional leaders. One moment he was fidgeting away, and the next moment there was an explosion, a hail of ancient splinters, and a loud thump as the Chief Executive sprawled at the feet of his astonished Vice President.

Perpetual motion has become a Kennedy signature, like Bourbon hemophilia or Borgia toxcity. Gore Vidal knew the ambassador's nine children when they were young. "I couldn't keep them straight," he remembers. "They were always running around like so many wirehaired terriers." "Whenever Teddy poked his head out the door," another friend of the family has remarked, "Jack would hit him with a pillow." With their father often away on deals and nine of them battling for the mother's attention, confusion was inevitable. Occasionally the family itself became muddled. To keep her children's medical and dental histories straight, Rose Fitzgerald Kennedy had to maintain a card index, and when she took them to the beach they had to wear identical bathing caps so she could keep track of them by counting heads. "The first time I remember meeting Bobby," the President has said in all seriousness, "was when he was three-and-a-half, one summer at the Cape."

When old Joe wasn't there, young Joe would act as a sort of deputy father. Being Kennedys, his brothers and sisters naturally vied with him, and intramurally his greatest rival was Jack, the next oldest. Over the years they fought the fiercest series of duels in the Kennedy record books; Bobby can still recall quailing with the girls while his big brothers slugged it out. "He had a pugnacious personality," the President has said of young Joe. "Later on it smoothed out, but it was quite a problem in my boyhood." In his late teens he still hadn't forgotten it. He picked Princeton partly because his brother had followed their father to Harvard, and though Jack changed his mind the next year, when the ambassador offered them trips abroad they went in opposite directions.

Yet while Jack defied young Joe, he also revered him. After the elder brother's death, those who knew him best — classmates, fellow officers, the family, and such friends of the family as Arthur Krock — contributed to a memoir, *As We Remember Joe*. Jack planned the book and selected as the envoi the lines from Maurice Baring: ". . . Our grief shall grow. For what can Spring renew/More fiercely for us than the need of you." The Kennedys instinctively compare scores in every activity; Bobby and Teddy followed Jack into the International News Service, and the ambassador has observed with a chuckle that "They even got married about the same time." But their sibling rivalry is only one side of the coin. The other face is a fierce tribal loyalty. Let one of them be threatened and the others hulk up, knuckles whitening. In pass patterns Bobby has no friends, he is all knees and elbows. Nevertheless he is the second man in the government today because, as one member of the kitchen cabinet explains it, "The President just naturally turns to him when he wants someone he can trust absolutely. This cuts across all lines; he will consult Bobby, not only on Justice affairs, but on any matter of importance." Joe's speculations notwithstanding, that feeling of kinship seems to be the natural outgrowth of continual parental supervision. That supervision did not stop when the brood achieved full growth. To the older Kennedys, the President's generation continued to be "the children"; Teddy, while an Assistant District Attorney and the father of two children of his own, remained "the baby." In the 1960's Rose and Joe persisted in vigil over what they still regarded as their nest. Perhaps Ted appeared on a Boston television channel and looked plump. In Hyannis Port they broke out the calorie charts and fired one off. Or perhaps the Attorney General of the United States was working too hard. He looked drawn. Georgetown began to gossip about it. Meanwhile, back at the ranch, his parents were already plotting to lure him away for a long weekend.

None of the boys has been watched more closely than young Joe's former sparring partner. Jack's arrival in postwar Washington was closely followed by the arrival of his mother, who wanted to check his rooms, and despite the separations from his father during his youth, Joe wrote him regularly, giving him pep talks via mail, lecturing him, and prodding him to improve his marks. When Jack was turning his Harvard thesis into a publishable manuscript — which he dedicated to his mother and father — the ambassador served as a second editor. From London he bombarded him with critiques,* and one of his passages appeared, almost intact, in the final version. In 1952 he was still exhorting him, this time egging him on against Henry Cabot Lodge, Jr.: "When you've beaten him, you've beaten the best. Why settle for something less?" Appointing Bobby as his campaign manager, Jack said wryly, "If I need somebody older there's no need to go outside the family. I can always get my father."

The ambassador would have been delighted. Unfortunately the appointment was out of the question. As the procession came out of the backstretch and approached the White House, Joe was obliged to withdraw into the background. For him this was an extremely difficult maneuver, but it was politic. Too many people remembered the years when he seemed to be an American Firster. He couldn't shut up entirely. Now and then he could be heard rumbling behind the scenes like a dormant volcano — "Not for chalk, money, or marbles will we take second place,"

* "You would be surprised how a book that really makes the grade with high-class people stands you in good stead for years to come," he wrote his son that summer. In April, 1961, Richard Nixon called on President Kennedy, who told him, in Nixon's words, that every public man should write a book "both for the mental discipline and because it tends to elevate him in popular esteem to the respected status of an 'intellectual.'" The visitor went off to write *Six Crises*, which shows how far Joe Kennedy's arm can reach.

he growled when it was suggested that his son settle for the Vice Presidency in 1960 — but most of the time he stayed put. His attitude toward entanglements abroad hasn't changed much. As the father of the Chief Executive he continued to be against foreign aid, and he confided that he thought trying to hold Berlin was "a bloody mistake." Long ago he and his most distinguished son agreed to disagree privately; there was little point in headlining their differences. After Jack's election to the Senate the ambassador would visit Washington just six hours a year, stopping off on his way north from Palm Beach to lunch with Krock, and between the installation of the new Administration and his disability nearly a year later he spent just one afternoon in the White House.

That doesn't mean he and his son aren't close. They are, very. Joe played a quiet but valuable campaign role in New York, New Jersey, and in Cook County, Illinois, where he has heavy holdings. During the Los Angeles convention he lurked nearby in Marion Davies's Beverly Hills mansion; only after the issue had been decided did he fly East, to watch, with Henry Luce, Jack's acceptance on television. After the election, father-son conversations eventually led to the President-Elect's two most important Cabinet choices, Dean Rusk and Robert McNamara, and the emotional bond remained strong. When Bobby phoned that the ambassador had been stricken, John Kennedy was visibly affected. Hanging up, he told an aide in a heavy voice, "Dad's gotten sick." The stroke interrupted an extraordinary presidential relationship. Until then the two had kept in almost constant touch by long-distance telephone. Joe had made a good sounding board, perhaps because the echo was so loud, and the President had called him as many as a half-dozen times a day, to argue, as they once did across the dinner table, about current events.

Under the unwritten rules of American politics it's not sporting to have an influential father. All relatives of officeholders are eyed dubiously. Blood lines are supposed to stop at the White House door. The ideal candidate is born in a Lincoln hut and orphaned as a child, after which he makes his way upward through snow and ice bearing a banner with the strange device *Ad astra per aspera,* or just *Per se.* In reality, these are the men who become sheriffs and selectmen. Most Presidents have families. Even Lincoln had one—*Dear Abe, I Received your Little check for 50.00 I shoed it to Mother She cried like a child,* read a letter which Dennis Hanks sent to 1600 Pennsylvania Avenue — and two Lincoln kin requested, and were granted, presidential patronage. No Kennedy needs a Little check for 50.00. This President's connections are better fixed than that one's were, which would have been bad had he abused his position on the way up. He didn't, unless campaign financing is admissible evidence, in which case a great many public men must stand in the dock. The only time he openly curried favor was when he decided to exchange stateside Navy duty for the sea, the Solomons, and the grimy cockpit of PT-109.

The father, in turn, might be indicted if he had tried to use his patriarchal power to dominate his son. Here the verdict is Scotch: not proven. Joe is undoubtedly a patriarch, but he himself took steps to counteract his own influence. He is an easy man to oversimplify, because he oversimplifies himself. His friendships with Hearst and Herbert Hoover suggest a stereotype, and then the stereotype disintegrates in the light of simultaneous ties with Jim Landis, Ben Cohen, William O. Douglas, and Tom Corcoran. He seems hidebound. Yet when his two oldest boys were still callow, he sent them to London to study under Harold Laski. Laski was a Socialist and an agnostic. In the ambassador's opinion he was also "a nut and a crank. I disagreed with everything he wrote. We were black and white. But I never taught the boys to disapprove of someone just because I didn't like him. They had heard enough from me, and I decided they should be exposed to someone of intelligence and vitality on the other side."

The exposure didn't take. Jack didn't turn pink, or even warm apricot. Defining his political hue has always been an exasperating task. The record reads any way you want it to read, depending on the tint of your own glasses. In one youthful letter he admired Italian fascism; in another he was critical of the Jesuits' role in Franco Spain. On Tulagi he argued that coconut plantation owners were entitled to compensation for trees damaged in the wear and tear of combat, a minority view at the time. Later, as a congressman, he became an enthusiastic supporter of Truman's domestic legislation — debating Taft-Hartley with young Nixon, and housing legislation with a still obscure Senator McCarthy — while he followed the G.O.P. line abroad on Yalta, Red China, and Owen Lattimore. He opposed Point Four, then circled the world in 1951 and decided to support it. He denounced the leaders of the American Legion as mossbacks and fought loyalty oaths, yet his record on anti-Communist witch-hunting was murky. His dedication to the Hoover Commission was so obvious, and his demands for economy in government so vehement, that many Massachusetts Republicans left their party to back him against Lodge. Later, as a presidential candidate, he sounded more like a Keynesian. Now, as President, he yearns, however vainly, for a balanced budget and has appointed Republicans to some forty sensitive posts in his Administration — meanwhile displaying rare courage in approaching the tariff nettle.

The Presidency subjects a man's past to dazzling light. "All the words he ever spoke or wrote, whether half asleep or wide awake, are exhumed and examined under circumstances to which they may no longer apply," Sidney Hyman wrote. Kennedy's critics have noted his public zigzags, and since he is not the only pungent politician, they have delivered some tart verdicts. One compared him to an elusive, light-weight, harum-scarum torpedo boat. A second suggested he show less profile and more courage. A third was reminded of Lord Bryce's opinion — cited in Allan Nevins's foreword to *Profiles* — that the American statesman "is apt to be timid in advocacy as well as infantile in suggestion." Kennedy himself has said of his early switch-hitting, "I'd just come out of my father's house at the time, and these were the things I knew." Unquestionably he was then aware of the ambassador's owlish eyes peering over his shoulder. Indeed, it can be argued that Joe felt quite safe in sending him to Laski, because he had already formed him. On the other hand, it may be held that sooner or later the cumulative effect of Harvard and European travel was bound to overwhelm the man who had made it all possible, and that, the President's academic friends are inclined to believe, is precisely what happened. According to them, the first stage of his career was a seesaw battle to free himself from his father's doctrines. In the mid-1950's, they contend, he severed the golden cord and became a liberal.

But he didn't become a Hubert Humphrey liberal. His brother Ted says that "He's a true liberal, approaching every problem with an open mind. How can you call a man a liberal if you can toss up a balloon and tell which way the wind's going to blow it for him?" It is true that the President seems quite free of prejudice. Unlike his father, he doesn't think of Jews as Jews, or call American Negroes "Lumumbas," or slight labor leaders. "Walter Reuther's wonderful," he told this writer when he discovered a common friendship there; "he's the last of the labor leaders with the old evangelical spirit." Nevertheless he can still sound the tory tocsin. Running across a magazine article critical of his Administration, he hurled it down and snapped, "What do these liberals want? Of course, I know. They want a deficit of seven billion dollars. Well, they should be happy. Berlin's going to cost us three and a half billion. That should bring enough pump-priming to satisfy them."

Harpoons from the left may hurt because he feels close to the harpooners. There is another explanation, however. Like many contemporaries, John Kennedy is impatient with all political gospels. Walter Lippmann, who seems to grow younger each year, spoke for the rising generation of Washington when he told the National Press Club that today "every truly civilized and enlightened man is conservative and liberal and progressive." Hardly anyone in the capital sounds the sectarian klaxons any more. They sound so flat, so meaningless. When the A.D.A. gives Thomas Dodd an eighty per cent liberal rating and barely passes William Fulbright with sixty per cent — these incredible scores were posted at the end of the first Kennedy year — A.D.A. shibboleths can no longer be treated seriously. Liberalism seems to belong to another time; perhaps in Spain of the early 1800's, when it first emerged under a party banner, as conservatism appeared in England thirty years later. "Liberal?

Conservative? I don't know what those labels mean," says Bobby Kennedy, shaking his head. The President himself hates to be pigeonholed. He prefers to quote Lincoln: "There are few things wholly evil or wholly good. Almost everything, especially of Government policy, is an inseparable compound of the two, so that our best judgment of the preponderance between them is continually demanded."

Asked what presidential label he expected to wear, Kennedy replied, "I hope to be responsible." He is an artist of the possible, an advocate of whatever will do the job. In his twenties he wrote that the British plan for Palestine seemed fair, and then added that justice wasn't enough; the need was for "a solution that will work." Searching for his own solutions in his forties, he follows no dogma, no dialectic, no theosophy. Carl Vinson once described him approvingly as "a practical young man," and one of the President's advisers says, "Actually he's always been a cautious politician." Yet he does like to get things done. To his wife he is an "idealist without illusions," which may be one way of calling him a pragmatist. The term isn't distasteful to him. "At least," he says, "we do things that work."

Like Jacqueline's historic curios, the belief that truth is tested by consequences finds its proper home in the White House. Despite its debt to British empiricism, pragmatism is an all-American philosophy. The word was coined by one Harvard man, C. S. Peirce, while another, William James, became the leader of the movement. William James would have enjoyed John Kennedy. They have more than ideas in common. James's health frequently failed him in his school years. During his youth his father's travels took the family to Europe, and that father — rich, ebullient, candid — had strong dynastic ambitions. It is of passing interest that the elder James fostered his paternal hopes by scorning business talk and encouraging lofty discussions at mealtimes, when he acted as moderator, teaching William, young Henry, and their fellow siblings how to debate. One family friend reported dinner arguments which grew so heated that the James boys brandished cutlery, but that sort of thing was unknown in the President's childhood. The Kennedys never used knives on each other. Joe would have thought it crude.

FIVE

Himself

THE PRESIDENT of the United States strides into the outer office, deftly skirts a spare rocker, and greets his visitor. It is now five months since the evening meeting which opened this book. John Kennedy is dressed as he was then, but his manner is much jauntier. The Administration's second winter is waning, and many of the burdens which seemed oppressive late in 1961 appear to be more tolerable. The Viet Cong are on the defensive, the American economy is strong, and censuring of military censorship has been discredited. At the moment the presidential mood is further boosted by a homely stimulant. It is a Saturday morning; at one o'clock he will join Jacqueline and the children for the weekend.

Yet as long as a Chief Executive remains here in the West Wing, it is the cockpit of action. Yesterday afternoon as the President talked with this writer his oval office was crisscrossed by aides. A door opened; Mac Bundy appeared with a dispatch. The knob turned again; Ted Sorensen was reporting. Saturdays should be quieter, but even now Evelyn Lincoln approaches.

"Yes, what's this?"

It is a document, it begs attention. He pauses to scan it and is, in that instant, framed against a background of framed photographs. The east wall, behind him, is a gallery of the great. There is one incongruity there. Among inscriptions from Harold Macmillan, Jawaharlal Nehru, and Douglas MacArthur — "with respect and admiration" — is a shelf bearing a gay piggy bank, a token of Caroline Kennedy's respect and admiration for Evelyn Lincoln. In a niche opposite are several snapshots of the donor. Like American bosses everywhere, the boss here enjoys displaying family memorabilia, and since he can't hang these prints in his own office he uses his secretary's.

The document read, the decision made, he leads the way into the oval office and closes the door.

The change is breathtaking. To an American no room in the world is so awesome. Partly this is a response to the Presidency — there can be no doubt where you are; the seal of the office is sculptured in the ceiling and repeated in the pattern of the gray rug below — and partly it is a submission to the spell of sheer beauty. The dimensions of the chamber are superb, appointments are exquisite, and the two wainscoted doors, when shut, blend into the wall, heightening the feeling of sanctum. Silence is absolute here; one thinks of a country estate, an illusion which is supported by the landscaping of the grounds outside. Looking out through the six French windows, each nearly twice as tall as a man, you see a vast reach of greenery and sky, and it takes a sharp eye to detect the unobtrusive White House policeman on the path beyond the rose garden. Today's sunlight is pale, lemon-colored. In another room it would be sickly, but filtered through the expanse of flawless glass it is almost streaming. Every detail of the office is clear: the naval paintings on the gently curving wall, the framed union jack, Commodore John Barry's sword, the ship model on the mantel, the intricate carving of the Victorian desk. Because of this light, and because all other tones are muted, the strong primary colors of the American and presidential flags are extraordinarily vivid, like those in an illuminated manuscript.

Flags and desk are at one end, the mantel at the other. On either side of the firescreen are facing sofas, slipcovered with a coarse beige fabric. Between them is a coffee table and the rocking chair. The President motions his visitor to the sofa on his right and sits in the rocker, facing the fireplace and cocking a foot on a slipcover. As though on signal his right hand begins to pluck absently at his tie. Then, as he talks, the hand drops to his knee, rises to stress a point, drops and rises again. His thoughts seem to come in rushes. He will comment; reflect briefly, as though weighing his own remarks; and then develop the comment. Very seldom does he avoid a topic, unless it involves security or — for the shield of reserve is always there — his privacy.

His conversation is versatile and, because of his penchant for detail, somewhat annotated. In a single meeting he deals with kinks in the balance of power, the Western Alliance, Asia, Africa, atomic testing, the Kremlin, the Eighty-seventh Congress. Domestic issues are broken down into automation, agriculture, medical care for the aged, the importance of being first in space, the difficulties of attracting gifted men to civil service, and, in an aside, the pleasant predicament of the bookies. Again and again he introduces the historical analogy, the Kennedy cachet: Vietnam is compared to postwar Greece, Berlin to postwar Austria, Korea to post-Punic War Rome, whose citizens were more sympathetic to police actions than twentieth-century Americans are.

It is an encyclopedic performance, and any writer who has condescended to climbers on the political ladder (while he himself has remained in journalism, which is more of a trampoline) is likely to feel a bit contrite. Occasionally the President's replies are vague, but he cannot be outfenced or outfoxed. Asked what he plans to do after his second term, he answers with a cagey grin that he doesn't yet know what he'll do after his *first* term. Then he concedes that "I was talking to Truman about this the other day," and — an example of the interviewee becoming the interviewer — he asks in turn, "What *do* ex-Presidents do?" Ex-President John Quincy Adams's return to the House of Representatives is mentioned, and his twenty-eighth successor swiftly points out, "Yes, but he made conditions. I doubt they'd be acceptable today."

Although a member of no party, Adams was appointed chairman of congressional committees, a practice which would be unthinkable now. Actually it is hard to say what would be acceptable in today's House. Thus far it has been a slough for John Kennedy. At times his legislative program has seemed to be an example of how to try in Congress without really succeeding. The President feels sanguine about the eventual fate of his big 1962 bills, and there are signs that the summer ahead may prove him right, but on the morning of this meeting the vote gap down the street is far more troubling than the missile gap he advertised in his campaign. Although he did secure housing, minimum wage, and foreign aid bills during the first session, he took more lumps than a honeymooning President should, and the second session opened with a barrage of rolling pins. Republicans claim that he is too clever. The real culprit seems to be the gerrymander, a pet of entrenched legislators and a monster to national leaders. Kennedy began his political career with faith in classical checks and balances, he being an entrenched congressman at the time. His yearning for a strong President came later, coincident with his yearning for the Presidency. In 1960 he called for strength, but the fickle public, while choosing him, decided at the same time to reject a score of representatives who would have seen things his way. He is a progressive President working with a Congress more conservative than Ike's. The early Sixties may, of course, mark the beginning of the end of diehard representation. With the Supreme Court ruling that urban citizens are entitled to appeal to federal courts if they aren't getting a fair shake from rural G.O.P. state legislatures, the character of those legislatures is expected to change. Since legislatures draw congressional districting lines, the House should change, too. But that lies far ahead. We are still in the season of the rotten borough. "Washington," John Kennedy once said lightly, "is a city of Southern efficiency and Northern charm." Rarely have the efficient Southern Democrats and the charming Northern Republicans dallied more successfully than in the first year of the Kennedy Administration. The spawn of the House womb was by Halleck out of Howard Smith, a union which proved to be exceedingly barren. The reactionaries, Reuther once charged, were "in bed together, hand in glove."

The President doesn't call it the do-nothing, good-for-nothing Eighty-seventh. He is, rather, unruffled. Joe Kennedy used to keep a sign on his desk reading,

After you've done your best, the hell with it. That, the ambassador maintained, "is the only sane point of view for any executive — including a Chief Executive." His son observes the legislative-executive tug-of-war with almost a bystander's curiosity. He ticks off the biases of individual congressmen and concludes, "There's nothing that can be done about a man from a safe district. He'll vote the way he wants to." The number of men straddling the fence at any given time is likely to be quite small. Of the five hundred and thirty-seven senators and representatives, less than a tenth are subject to persuasion on a vital bill. So the branches duel: "You've always had tension between the White House and the Hill," he says quietly, "and you always will."

What was, is; what is, will be. That is the Kennedy acceptance, the line of departure. He does not stop there, of course, but none of the changes he proposes would raze the frame we know. As he tots up world events since his inaugural, one is struck by his sense of historical continuity. The path he follows is illumed by familiar beacons at his back. His context is the world in being, which, to the jaundiced, means negativism, "no-win." If you pick your issues, you can build a case for that. On many fronts he is frankly defending the status quo. Thus the absence of a Laotian collapse is cause for cheer. The Congo chess game is going well, for there is a chance of stability and no American troops have been committed. The fact that the U.N. did not fall apart after Dag Hammarskjold's death inspires optimism, the Berlin wall is a point for our side since it was a confession of Red failure, and the Cuban carcinoma is less unsightly now that more and more Latin Americans realize Castro is a bad lot. No-win, in sum, is no-lose; they also serve who only stand and wait.

To leave the President there, however, would be to foul him. Every leader, even an insurgent, must fight some holding actions. John Kennedy does not see success in the absence of failure. He sees it where Fourth of July orators used to say they saw it — in the export of the American Revolution. For Kennedy there are no lesser breeds without the law; to him our eighteenth-century seeds are still viable, and sowable in almost any soil. He believes, as John Foster Dulles did not believe, that newly free nations have the right to true independence. Krishna Menon's manners are annoying but irrelevant; when neutral governments are rude the President doesn't go off and sulk. He prefers to dwell on a conversation with Nehru, who told him that while in prison during World War II he received a message of encouragement from Franklin Roosevelt. Nehru treasures that memory, John Kennedy thinks it a good thing he does, and his program is designed to spread the same encouraging light to other lands. He means to befriend them and help them, which, in a nutshell, is the argument for long-term economic loans.

"We have this foreign aid fight every year," he says. In the wan sunlight of this Saturday forenoon, the

Capitol again looms large; money bills must come out of the lower House, which the Constitution entrusted with the national cash register. And once more his tone is matter-of-fact, accepting. America's heritage is the American President's trust, though the modifications of nearly two centuries are as important to him as the words of the founding fathers. Reminded that James Madison favored congressional control over foreign policy, he shakes his head vigorously. "That would be unthinkable today. You couldn't have divided authority and still be free. Time has changed a great many things. The executive has grown so; the legislative branch looks to the executive for leadership. But there are also congressional institutions which were not anticipated by the founding fathers. For example, the seniority system was not foreseen." He rubs his knee. "The system does seem to work this way, and there seems to be an inevitability about it." Of his own Administration he holds that "My relations with Congress are satisfactory. They will continue to be satisfactory if I'm strong in the country."

Yet what kind of strength does the country want? President Kennedy is reminded of Senator Kennedy's concern about American flaccidity. He and the men around him pointed out that prosperous societies tend to sink into apathy. Those to whom much is given rarely feel the obligation to give anything in return; a nation glued to Huckleberry Hound cannot hear the audio of clarion calls. Machiavelli pointed out that it was "necessary that Moses should find the people of Israel slaves in Egypt and oppressed by the Egyptians, so that they were disposed to follow him in order to escape from their servitude." Machiavelli's stark logic is unanswerable: no discontent, no Moses. If a people lack any sense of oppression, what value can a pragmatist find in their esteem?

Kennedy smiles. "Naturally a President must be willing to lose some of his popularity. Far better that than do as Coolidge did — go out in a blaze of glory and leave a time bomb."

The President motions his visitor to remain. Opening a French window he stands by it a moment, enjoying the dank air; then, abruptly, he throws his shoulders back, revealing the blue *JFK* on his shirt. It is an exuberant gesture, and as he returns to his rocker the writer remarks that the Kennedy glory has never blazed more brightly; the latest Gallup poll has given him a favorable rating of eighty-two per cent. Does he feel any sense of compassion for the plight of the Republican party?

The President's reply is negative, and somewhat salty. Indeed, he feels so little compassion that his visitor feels obliged to explain. It can be argued that the Republicans may eventually join such political ghosts as the Know-Nothings, the Anti-Masons, the Barnburners, and the Locofocos. This morning the G.O.P. holds just sixteen of fifty governorships, thirty-six of one hundred senatorial seats, 174 of 437

House seats. The voters are heavily Democratic; at last count fewer than two of every five preferred the minority party. Over the past three decades Republicans have controlled Congress for just four years — despite Eisenhower's appeal, three of his four congresses were led by the opposition — and the general was elected as a war hero, not as a party man. Omitting him, there hasn't been a Republican Chief Executive since 1933. For most of the last thirty years the history of the G.O.P. has been gloom and doom.

"I'll give *you* the history of the last *hundred* years." The right hand darts up. "Except for Roosevelt, the century has been dominated by Republicans. Who were the other Democrats? There was Cleveland. There was Wilson — who was reelected to his second term by one of the narrowest of margins. Truman's margin was tiny, too, and so was mine. A shift of a few votes in 1960 and they'd be in here. They can take any issue — Laos, South Vietnam — and try to ride it to the top. What throws the congressional figures off, and those of the state houses, is the Democratic South."

Still, there is that Galluping eighty-two per cent. The figure is both imposing and perplexing. Truman's margin dwindled sharply after his slender victory, but Kennedy is outscoring the idols, Roosevelt and Eisenhower; he even gets Pulliam fan letters from intransigent Republican Indiana. The President has pondered this, and pinching fingers he counts off what he believes to be the reasons for his prestige. "First there is the national respect for the Presidency. Formerly I was seen as a partisan figure and a Catholic. Now they see me as President. Second, my desires are those of most of the American people. Third, people sense that we face terribly difficult problems — the fact that after Cuba I took full responsibility, and that we haven't gotten into serious trouble, are factors here. Finally, I don't attempt to run the office on a partisan basis. Truman did; he could. I can't. I need support for the Common Market, for example, and in the Congo. That's more important than a partisan exchange. I have to have the Congress behind me. I can't alienate them."

Kennedy seldom alienates anyone deliberately, and that, the poll takers have found, is one reason for his appeal. At home he tries to avoid what he calls "a highly charged political position"; abroad he is correct and attentive, a sort of one-man listening post. Of the inscribed photographs in the next room he says, "Contacts with other chiefs of state don't alter the basic structure; they can't change a culture. They *do* make relationships easier. And they help you determine how events are going to go. A talk may not settle anything. Often it appears fruitless. But later you can make a more realistic judgment of reactions. In that sense even the Vienna meeting was useful, although it eased no tensions, because it permitted, at least on my part, a more precise estimate of Mr. Khrushchev's intentions."

Other Presidents could be swashbucklers, but "that

is no guide. There is no valid comparison with the past. Our era is even different from Truman's. In Truman's time we had the bomb, we were supreme. During the decade from '45 to '55 our relative power was so much greater. It wasn't until the last two years of Eisenhower's second term that the balance really shifted. This is something that every President from now on must face. Because the balance has changed, we're challenged in so many areas — in Laos, in Vietnam, in Haiti . . ." His hand opens slowly, suggesting a world of challenges. "We simply must reconcile ourselves to the fact that a total solution is impossible in a nuclear age."

Americans have been bred to think otherwise. Our history fosters the belief that we can do anything, and quickly, too. De Tocqueville found us the least philosophical of creatures. A few moral saws served us well enough. Our driving force has been an impatient energy — "We are," wrote Henry Wallace, "a people given to excesses." That ginger conquered the old frontier, and John Kennedy's let's-go version of it brought his own frontier to the Potomac. But the atom, Albert Einstein warned, requires a new way of thinking. Our ancestors' maxims already seem rather quaint. Davy Crockett's, about making sure you're right and then going ahead, is as useless as modern thrift plans are thriftless. The philosopher Glenn Gray suggests that we have abandoned pioneer morality and are groping toward something else, that Puritan notions of right and wrong are being replaced by a Hellenic sense of the fitness of things. And indeed, we do appear to be less interested in rectitude than in suitability; Panmunjom taught us that in war there really is a substitute for victory. The Air Force watchword — "The difficult we do immediately, the impossible takes a little longer" — is a relic of the pre-air age. The impossible is literally impossible now. More temperate slogans are suggested for the Sixties: Talleyrand's "Above all, no zeal," or Thucydides' "Men do what they can, and suffer what they must."

The John Birch Society doesn't intend to take this lying down. It has no relevance to Americanism as hundred per cent Americans know it. Birchers believe in standing tall and thinking big; they remember Valley Forge and the Alamo, and red blood courses through their veins. Lately they and their fellow rightists — Christian Crusaders, Circuit Riders, Liberty Lobbyists, National Indignation Rallies — have been enjoying a marginal vogue. The Cuban folly, like Britain's Suez fiasco, aroused votaries of good old-time patriotism. The clearer the new way of thinking becomes, the more the lunatic fringe frays; Pierre Salinger, who is as American as pizza, has actually been accused of being "the head of the Communist conspiracy in the United States." Each month new species of Americanists debouch from the woodwork with combat-ready tape recorders and advance grimly, denouncing the United Nations, the continent of Africa, and one another.

The President's response to these angry Americans

is typically rational. He merely observes that the world is complex and dangerous, that rightists yearn for simplicity and safety, and that they err. "Radical solutions won't work," he says, shifting in his chair, "but there is a gradual, evolutionary process. Events are moving all the time, whether or not we are aware of them. Take this dissension in the Communist system — the China split, Albania. We couldn't have predicted it, and here it is. In my judgment we should guide the right processes in a variety of ways. We are doing that by binding ourselves more closely to the Atlantic community in economic matters, by helping the United Nations build a world of free states that can maintain their freedom, and, in South America, through the *Alianza*. The *Alianza* is evolutionary, but in the long run it will add up to the same thing as a revolution." He rocks a moment. "There isn't any magic in it. Our purpose is to prevent the balance of power from swinging to the Communist bloc. You maintain your position and hope that eventually there will be enough fission in their society."

Really the Pro-Blues are a Republican problem — as Wallace, fourteen years ago, was a threat to Democrats. The money the ultras aren't contributing to G.O.P. campaigns is money they wouldn't have contributed to the New Frontier anyhow. Yet Kennedy's waiting game is also repugnant to enthusiasts in his own camp; the *Reporter* has been as glum as the *National Review*. There is this difference: Democratic idealists counted on more. Except for the Custer's

Last Stand Stevensonians, most Northern Democrats backed Jack in 1960. The intelligentsia, which is as vital to the Democratic party as industrialists are to Republicans, was jubilant at his triumph. Their expectations were at least as great as the Old Guard's had been in 1953. Kennedy, they noted approvingly, solicited the opinions of certified experts and listened attentively. Those who were close to him should have realized that meant nothing. In campaigns he often asked reporters' advice and rarely took it. But the intellectuals — including a number of newspapermen — soared above facts. Their man was in the White House, and they weren't going to let anything spoil the party.

Then came Cuba, the soggy blanket. Pig Bay shocked them. The rightists denounced the President for failing to provide air cover. The scholastics couldn't understand how he could have bought such a vulgar plan; Chet Bowles wouldn't have touched it. By summer they were rushing Cassandra assessments of the Kennedy Presidency to the printer. "Why?" Ted Kennedy asked in December. "The time to judge this Administration is three years from now." Ted was prejudiced, but he had a point. It seemed a trifle early to write his brother off. The crux of power is timing. For a politician, wrote the author of *Profiles in Courage*, "to decide at which point and on what issue he will risk his career is a difficult and soul-searching decision." Able leaders know how to wait, and when to strike. The greatest Ameri-

can Presidents have been better at landings than
take-offs. Theodore Roosevelt and Woodrow Wilson
didn't make their marks until their second terms, and
at the end of Lincoln's first year his major accomplish-
ments were the passage of the first Legal Tender
Act and the total disruption of the Union.

Nevertheless, after Cuba the flak of criticism thick-
ened. Joseph Rauh of the A.D.A. summed up the liberal position: "Compared to the high hopes we had,
he's a bitter disappointment." The more Kennedy's
Gallup percentage waxed, the more insistent were the
demands that he convert it into achievement. How
could he do it? He certainly couldn't convert it all.
Apart from Franklin Roosevelt's first three months in
the mansion, few Presidents have been able to bring
the full weight of their prestige to bear upon events.
Harry Truman snorted, "I sit here all day trying to
persuade people to do the things they ought to have
sense enough to do without my persuading them."
Still, Truman managed to do a lot of persuading when,
according to Gallup, only twenty-three per cent of
the American people approved of him. As Kennedy entered his second year he wore the aura of a
matinee idol, yet progress along his Frontier was
spotty. "Certainly he's got the country going again,"
one presidential aide said defensively. "Look what
Minow's done to TV programing." Examinations of
the economy and the Atlantic alliance suggested a
more favorable verdict than that, but the political
scientists and the capital pros were unconsoled. At

cocktail parties you heard worn jokes about "the third
Eisenhower Administration," caustic digs at the
President's brothers and brothers-in-law, complaints
about lack of vision. Obviously Georgetown was disillusioned.

Georgetown was disillusioned, the public content.
There was irony here. No one had understood the difference between general approbation and the sanc-
tion of experts better than candidate Kennedy; none
had seen more clearly the justice in the professionals'
laments. His own offices were peopled with men who
had wrung their hands over Eisenhower apathy and
craved leadership. Privately some of them have
shared the disappointment of the cocktail circuit. This
one blamed the legacy of events. That one thought
the President's concept of national leadership was
limited by his senatorial experience, that in press conferences he appeared to be unaware of the vast, un-
sophisticated audience of television eavesdroppers. A
third brooded over America's mood, her sullen re-
fusal to recognize her peril. "It was the best of times,
it was the worst of times," wrote a parliamentary reporter named Dickens. "It was the spring of hope, it
was the winter of despair, we had everything before
us, we had nothing before us. . . ."

The President's liberal scolds were demanding un-
remitting boldness — as though boldness would convert Wilbur Mills, Jim Delaney, or Howard Smith —
and they wanted plenty of gunsmoke. Many of them
felt that he should have staked everything on thwart-

ing John McCormack's yearning for the Speakership. He would have gained respect, they contended, even if he had failed. "That," a presidential adviser agrees, "was one time Kennedy would have fought if he'd thought he had a gambler's chance of winning." But there was no chance. Every congressional barometer indicated that he would have been certain to fail. The President's only achievement would have been a loss of face, and in politics there is no solace in defeat. So divorced from reality was the McCormack-shall-not-pass argument that its explanation must lie elsewhere. "The fact is, of course, that no successful President could satisfy the intellectual's longing for logical, uncompromising purity," a contributor to the *American Scholar* conceded. "In the White House, as in baseball, 'nice guys finish last.'"

Perhaps the key to the purists' disenchantment lies in their political weaning. Most of the reigning ideologues left their teens in the heyday of the New Deal. For them the name Roosevelt has a special magic; it lures them toward a sentimental journey into the past. We are accustomed to conservative necromancy. Both Eisenhower and Robert A. Taft, in different ways, attracted those who pined for a vanished America — for long shirttails, celluloid collars, flypaper, whalebone corsets, harvest home suppers, and the benevolent paternalism of the Cleveland Business Men's Marching Club. Today that longing has been matched by a liberal nostalgia, which winds its mournful horn in the breasts of those who look back with sad affection to the Great Depression, when they were children, and liberalism was a viable crusade, and Fala was alive, wagging his little tail.

"Of course there is a yearning for the Thirties," says the President, nodding vehemently. "It's only natural. Every generation remembers its youth." He cites an elderly Washington columnist who still laments the departure of Wilsonian idealism, and adds, "Perhaps in another ten years we'll have another period we hark back to. But nostalgia is particularly characteristic of the New Deal liberals right now."

He bears some responsibility for their hangovers. The all-out enthusiasm of J.F.K.'s first weeks — the late nights, the manic mood — and the influx of professors inevitably evoked memories of F.D.R., and at the outset the President encouraged reminiscence. He had announced that his first months would be patterned after the Hundred Days of 1933. Like Roosevelt he decorated his office with maritime mementos. Schlesinger, the New Deal historian, was brought into the government. The organization (or disorganization) of the White House took the press corps back a quarter-century; some of the older correspondents thought even Kennedy's mannerisms were like Roosevelt's. Washington took its cue accordingly. Vice President Johnson of Texas was compared to Vice President Garner of Texas, and it was duly noted that Benjamin Cohen, Thomas Corcoran, James H. Rowe, Jr., Abe Fortas, and Mrs. Anna Rosenberg, all old New Dealers, were advising Johnson. Carl Sandburg announced that Kennedy was "a little more like F.D.R. than any other President." The new Chief Executive's breakfasts in bed and his skimming of the morning papers were quickly tagged as Rooseveltian. Raymond Moley dwelt on the "likeness in self-confidence, activism, and personal charm"; in Kennedy, as in Roosevelt, he wrote, "there is love of power and authority and intense ambition." Even Arthur Krock reverted to the crabby old Krock of yesteryear, and when Sorensen, who works on presidential speeches, became known as "the Sam Rosenman of the staff," and the President's pleasantries with Dirksen and Halleck were compared to Roosevelt's friendships with Charlie McNary and Joe Martin, the reincarnation seemed complete. All that was lacking was word that spectral Bourbons had gone to the Trans-Lux to hiss Kennedy.

The word never came. The parallel had been badly drawn. Temperamentally President Kennedy has far less in common with President Roosevelt than has, say, Nelson Rockefeller, and as he himself belatedly points out, "The two eras are entirely different. Roosevelt's problems were wholly domestic; mine are largely foreign. There is no validity to the comparison." Nevertheless, those for whom the F.D.R. image was explicit have clung to it, and in their fervor some of them have created a Roosevelt who never existed. "They forget that he was such a showoff and dissembler," says James M. Burns, who has published studies of both Presidents. "They remember the Hundred Days, the second Hundred Days, the 1936 election, the court pack — to show that the hero stumbled — and then the coming of the war. But they skip over the second term, when F.D.R. had a very tough time. In 1936, 1937, and 1938 he was overcome by obstacles. This was the time of the recession; everything was going badly for him. They don't remember that in those years he was evasive, noncommittal, exasperatingly cautious — and the despair of the intellectuals." That despair had, in fact, become manifest even before the end of the first term, when the father of a Harvard freshman denounced the Administration's denouncers. After excoriating the Birchers of the time, Joseph P. Kennedy observed that "On the opposite front, the New Deal is assailed by melancholy radicals who want so many things, and want them done overnight."

As a realist John Kennedy shares his father's distrust of political romantics, and as an historian he is equipped to ambush those who distort the past. Toward the end of one White House meeting a New York editor accosted him. "Let me tell you what I think you should do," he said waspishly. "You should go on the radio every week, like F.D.R., and tell the people —"

The President interrupted him. "Roosevelt went on the radio every week?"

"That's right," said the editor, "for his weekly fireside chat."

In cool riposte Kennedy informed him that during

welve years in office Franklin D. Roosevelt delivered
ust twenty-seven fireside chats, an average of less
than one every five months, and that the maximum
in any year was four.

To ardent admirers the master of such minutiae
naturally appears to be a mastermind. "Back in '46 we
knew that if we exposed him for a ten-minute coffee
session we'd pick up a high percentage of volunteer
workers," says Lem Billings, who works on Madison
Avenue. "I've often thought that if we had a product
to advertise on television with that kind of a return,
we'd get fantastic results." Yet the question of the
President's intellect does have another side. "Intellectually he's committed," Burns says; "emotional commitment is a different matter, though. The people
who want a fighting President do have an argument.
Think of Harry Truman in 1948. He just plugged
away down the line for what he believed in, and he
happened to win. Kennedy has been wonderful at
communicating ideas, but he hasn't communicated
anything like the Truman image of '48. I wonder how
much he will be loved by the people, in the Lincoln
sense. Liked — yes. But loved?"

Certainly John Kennedy is not as lovable as Abe.
He has a weaker grip on the nation's heartstrings, and
the reason isn't that he hasn't been shot. One explanation is posited in the area; the lonely crowd is shy of
affection. Another, however, is inherent in the man
himself. The President's response to his public is

that of an intrigued window-shopper, or an inquisitiv
reporter. His mind is so literal that at times he seem
to lack the capacity to generalize — to kindle all th
facts and set them ablaze. It is a remarkable fact tha
he approved the censure of Joe McCarthy, not be
cause McCarthyism offended him, but because h
merely thought the senator had been out of orde
Campaigning in Little Rock, he was asked what h
would do if he became President, and he astounde
his audience by giving them a specific, point-by
point account of the steps a Chief Executive coul
take. No visionary flights; just a cold blueprint. Again
this writer inquired of him whether one of his publi
remarks ("I feel that the Adams family intimidate
us all. . . .") meant that a President with a sense o
history is inclined to judge himself against President
of the past. The reply was a cogent analysis of th
strengths of the Adams family.

Some see this trait as a weakness. It need not be
Caesar and Napoleon shared it. The reluctance to
enter into meditative penumbrae means the absence
of dogma, which in turn means calm, good-humored
relations with men all along the political spectrum. It
need not even fault him intellectually. "Remember,
Toynbee is not the only philosopher of history," an
old Kennedy acquaintance observes. "The President
doesn't resemble him much, but he has a lot in common with Sir Lewis Namier — and, for that matter,
with Tacitus."

Anxius et intentus agere. "Always active, never im-

ulsive." As the first anniversary of Kennedy's in-
uguration came and went Tacitus (55?–after 117
.D.) seemed to be the real Schlesinger of his Ad-
ninistration. He struck closer to the bone than Machi-
velli, de Tocqueville, Thucydides, or Joe Alsop. The
'resident remained in perpetual motion, prodding
Vashington drones, poring over diplomatic cables, ac-
osting his staff Monday mornings with sheafs of
ables hacked from Sunday papers. He moved swiftly,
et it was all deliberate speed. Privately he seethed
ver Republican sniping at his foreign policy, but he
arely mounted a counterattack; he called, rather,
or nonpartisan solidarity. Abroad he navigated an
xtremely narrow channel, and Everett McKinley
Dirksen was his co-pilot. In a jam, he reached for the
lag. After Cuba he consulted Eisenhower, Hoover,
MacArthur, Nixon, Rockefeller, and Goldwater, a
pectacle which displeased Democratic partisans but
pleased the country. The words he entered into the
ecord were carefully weighed; you couldn't im-
igine him dashing off a savage note to a critic of Caro-
ine's voice. He cherished Bulwer-Lytton's maxim,
'When it is not necessary to change it is necessary
not to change," and the moves he did make were preceded by elaborate card-file preparation and a realistic appreciation of the limits of government. *Omnia
scire, non omnia exsequi.* "He knew all, though he
did not always act upon all he knew."

Aging liberals were unreconciled — the capital still
buzzed with talk of fireside chats, take-it-to-the-peo-

ple campaigns, "appeals to the nation." None of i
came from 1600 Pennsylvania Avenue. The right also
thundered on — "We need a man on horseback," a
rootin tootin Texan told the President, "and many
people think you are riding Caroline's tricycle." John
Kennedy wouldn't sit that sort of horse well. Robert
Frost advised him that "Poetry and power is the for-
mula for an Augustan age," and in reply he received
a scrawled, "Power all the way." Yet the President
didn't mean the tub-thumping power of a Castro. He
is just not that kind of man. "Regardless of the iden-
tities of those who will occupy the White House in
the years to come," his father wrote in *I'm for Roosevelt*, the problems would require "self-restraint."
That quality was inconspicuous in both the bombas-
tic ambassador and the bantam cock he was then
championing. John Kennedy, on the other hand, is
anti-histrionic by nature. He hates to be a bore. He
hasn't the egomania of those who never doubt that
the masses are panting to hear them. And at his age
he's not likely to become a flamboyant, happy warrior.

But he is a warrior: a man whose life reveals great
physical valor and fierce, inscrutable drives. To the
blustering Texan he replied frostily, "Wars are easier
to talk about than they are to fight. I'm just as tough
as you are, and I didn't get elected President by
arriving at soft judgments." While a large part of his
success may be put down to prudent calculation, he
has made the tough choice too often to be dismissed
as a trimmer. In his first campaign he was the only

*ndidate to back Truman's British loan, and his sup-
ort of the St. Lawrence Seaway led New England
ewspapers to the conclusion that he was committing
enatorial suicide. As a presidential aspirant he raised
he religious issue despite protests from his staff; as
resident-Elect he ignored State Department advice
nd responded warmly to Khrushchev's congratula-
ory message; as President he made the politically in-
xpedient decision to close some seventy military in-
tallations and raised the banner of free trade, which
n opportunist, remembering Cleveland, would have
ept tightly furled. He honors the heroic tradition;
ne of his Republican friends believes that Richard
Jixon's irresolute behavior during their race de-
troyed him in Kennedy's eyes. "I remember him say-
ng in 1956 that if anything happened to Ike, the
ountry would be in good hands," Jim Reed says. "But
e admires courage, and he feels that Nixon was pusil-
animous in 1960 — especially in the first debate,
vhere he kept saying, 'I agree with you.' He had ex-
ected Nixon to stand up to him, and was contemp-
uous of him when he didn't."

Sometimes a single chain of events discloses the
haracter of a leader with chain-lightning clarity.
Andrew Jackson's flashing response to South Carolin-
an tariff defiance, Andrew Johnson's tactless blun-
ders after the Tenure of Office Act, Theodore Roosevelt's swift support of Panamanian secession, Harding's Alaskan panic — each sequence has left a vivid

impression of a man caught in the lens of time. Fo
John Kennedy such an illumination came in the
fifteenth month of his Presidency, when, for seventy
two hours, he was tested in the Bessemer heat of the
Big Steel challenge.

The test began with a bland question at four o'clock
on the afternoon of Tuesday, April 10, 1962. Ken
O'Donnell's West Wing telephone rang, and on the
other end was a spokesman for Roger M. Blough,
chairman of the board of the United States Steel Cor-
poration. The chairman was flying to Washington;
could he see the President? O'Donnell had no idea
what was up, but he was cordial. Blough was a familiar figure in the mansion. Two weeks before, the
steel industry and the steelworkers' union had signed
a contract which had been heralded as a dike against
inflation, and the Chief Executive, whose prestige
had become deeply committed during the negotiations, had praised it as "industrial statesmanship of
the highest order." O'Donnell set the appointment
for 5:45 P.M.

In the oval office it was an exceptionally quiet afternoon. Kennedy thought he might even have time
for a book. Double-checking, he asked Mrs. Lincoln
whether he was in the clear.

"You have Mr. Blough at a quarter to six," she told
him.

"Mr. Blough?"

"Yes."

The President was puzzled. "Get me Kenny O'Donnell."

O'Donnell confirmed it, and shortly before six the steel chairman entered the oval office. Kennedy waved him to the right-hand sofa, sat in the rocker, and waited.

"Perhaps the easiest way to explain why I am here is to give you this and let you read it," Blough said, handing him a four-page press release.

The mimeographed handout — it was already on its way to the newspapers — announced that his firm was boosting the price of steel six dollars a ton. The action itself was shocking, and the manner in which the President was informed suggested a deliberate, sandbagging snub. "I think you have made a terrible mistake," he told Blough stonily. He instructed Mrs. Lincoln to fetch Secretary Goldberg. The three of them talked for fifty minutes, and after Blough departed five aides were summoned. Pacing the floor, the President tautly recalled a row between Joe Kennedy and steel executives in 1937. At the time he had believed that his father's denunciations of them were exaggerated.* Now he understood. For now his blood

* In a version published by the New York *Times* on April 23, 1962, the President was quoted as having said, "My father always told me that all businessmen were sons-of-bitches but I never believed him till now!" Although Orvil E. Dryfoos, publisher of the *Times*, wrote a letter to the President apologizing for this, the rendering was widely circulated. It inspired a great deal of indignation in the business community and, in some quarters, a show of hypocritical dismay. For example, an Oklahoma City news-

was up. His urbane mask was off; he was on collision course. "U. S. Steel picked the wrong President to double-cross," one aide said afterward. "Six o'clock, six o'clock," Kennedy muttered to himself as that evening's guests entered the White House at 9:45. They were in black tie; the occasion was his annual reception for members of Congress. Just a year before, he had been drawn aside and told of the Pig Bay disaster, and tonight he remarked dryly, "I think we're going to call off congressional receptions. Last year it was Cuba, now this."

Wednesday at breakfast he heard reports from economists and statisticians who had worked almost all night, gathering data. Then he told Sorensen to begin drafting a statement. His hope was to head off U. S. Steel's competitors. It seemed vain. By afternoon, when he mounted his press conference rostrum, five of them, led by Bethlehem Steel, had matched Blough's increase. A thoroughly aroused President faced the reporters. While the members of Blough's high command glowered at a television set twenty stories above Manhattan's Broadway, he gibbeted them with language which made "economic royalists" sound almost benign. Citing particulars to show the new prices were unjustified, he warned of antitrust investigations, the cancellation of proposed tax benefits for industry, and the loss of defense orders.

paper piously headed a story, "JFK Used Bad Words in Steel Crisis," and described the operative phrase as "gutter language." Yet this language enjoyed a splendid vogue in the same newspaper's city room when this writer inhabited it.

This was onstage. Backstage, New Frontiersmen with steel friends were telephoning them, trying to persuade the companies which hadn't raised rates to stay put. As a member of the staff said later, "Anybody who knew anybody else got on the horn." Switchboards were ablaze, for a lot of people knew people — the vice chairman of Inland Steel received an early morning greeting from the Undersecretary of Commerce, a fellow old boy of Chicago's Harvard School for Boys ('23), and one steel man was proselytized by four members of the Administration. Secretary McNamara sat at his desk, personally dialing number after number; the President himself made innumerable calls, notably one to Edgar Kaiser, chairman of Kaiser Steel, in California. Meanwhile Bobby had a posse of FBI agents prowling the night, routing out reporters to verify a quotation from Bethlehem's president opposing a price hike.

"Gestapo tactics!" cried the chairman of the Republican National Committee, and the pro-steelie *Wall Street Journal*, discovering that one of its men had been awakened by Bobby's dawn patrol, was fit to be tied. Beyond doubt the President was using the full powers of his office. And beyond doubt they were working. Thursday Roger Blough conceded that if his competitors didn't follow his lead he would be in a fix. Already five of them were wavering, two seriously. Friday morning the U. S. Steel chairman called Secretary Goldberg. Roger was doing a twist. His people were going to have a quiet little talk in New

York, he said; would the Secretary like to sit in? Goldberg accepted and then phoned the President for advice. Kennedy's terms were simple: unconditional surrender. The conclave was held secretly in uptown New York's Carlyle Hotel, with Goldberg and Clark Clifford present, but even as Clifford was lecturing the company men their hopes for a united industry were fading. First Blough was called to the phone, then Goldberg. Inland Steel and Kaiser had broken ranks — in Washington the President said, "Good! Good! Very good!" — and their abstention had forced Bethlehem to recant. At a quarter after five that same afternoon Blough tossed in the towel. This time there was no handout. The news of Kennedy's victory came over an AP teletype in the West Wing and was relayed by Sorensen to Norfolk, Virginia, where the President was watching naval maneuvers. Hearing it as he debarked from a nuclear submarine, he announced that the people were "most gratified," and that Big Steel was now "serving the public interest." The three-day blitz was over.

Fascinated by Kennedy's display of presidential pyrotechnics, most Americans missed the revealing display of Himself. It was all there. U. S. Steel's unexpected flaunting of the Jolly Roger brought out the President's competitive drive, his wit in adversity, his reliance on Bobby, and his instinctive turning, in tense moments, to thoughts of his father. The Wednesday statement, edited by him moments before its presentation, confirmed his affinity for detail and his sense of history — certain passages evoked rhythms of T.R., F.D.R., and Woodrow Wilson. The phone calls to Establishment magnates demonstrated the recherché tone of his government. Finally, in choosing to counterattack he had remained the canny politician. Big Steel has little appeal in the nation; the Republicans, who defended the tycoons, were following their fatal instinct for the impolitic.*

Undeniably the crisis changed him. Crises do shape a President, and may, in time, completely transform him — at the end of their Administrations Herbert Hoover and Harry Truman were very different men. At this writing it would be hazardous, even presumptuous, to predict the ultimate effect of the office on John Kennedy. In the rumbles ahead, each of his qualities will be tempered, smashed, or recast. Clearly the second week of April, 1962, fortified the President's sense of confidence; it strengthened his feeling of the country, and the country's feeling for him. It further fused his political faith; until then, no one had realized how deeply he believed in economic planning. This was the most conspicuous harvest of Blough's seed, and it incited extravagant reactions. The steelsymps promptly developed delusions of persecution; within two months they had raised such a

---

* The fact that the President's popularity dropped four points after the steel fight merely demonstrates that when a leader strikes out in *any* direction he always leaves a few stragglers. Those who follow this numbers game noted that Kennedy was still nearly ten points above Eisenhower's average rating, and nearly thirty above Truman's. Actually he should shed more popularity fat. Inevitably he will.

convincing bogy that the stock market threw a major convulsion. For them the discovery that Kennedy meant business with business overrode everything else — a financial writer charged that he had thrown an "anti-business tantrum." Humbler men were thrilled — "Oh, didn't he do a good one!" exclaimed a delighted Robert Frost, adding that "Somebody's got to get angry."

Actually both had missed the essence of him. A show of strength is not wrath. It was true, as one White House aide put it, that his Tuesday mood was "controlled fury." Certainly he was indignant. In the face of such provocation no man could have remained serene. What was remarkable, however, was the control. During that first session in the oval office Goldberg flew at Blough, but Kennedy, though arctic, was civil. There was no Truman stridor in his press conference thrust; it was delivered with the hard, measured cadence of a judge pronouncing sentence on the perpetrators of a particularly inexcusable crime. He gnawed no carpets, he didn't foam, he avoided the "highly charged political position." Even before U. S. Steel struck its colors he was warning his staff that "it is very important that we not take any action that could be interpreted as vindictive"; and when the firm's chairman requested another appointment four days later ("This," said the voice on the other end of the horn, "is Roger Blough, the man you've been reading about"), he was received graciously, the guest of a Chief Executive still anxious for his cooperation. Like Goethe, John Kennedy believes that genius lies in knowing where to stop. He had shown the mailed fist, and then he had sheathed it in deepest velvet. Once more he was himself, the quiet American.

In every emergency, so the democratic faith goes, the United States finds a President capable of taking arms against her sea of troubles. The Georgetown quarterbacks, despite their momentary elation over the steel triumph, continue to distrust Kennedy's tranquillity. They want him to adopt the iron tone every day, everywhere. Like the Circuit Riders and the Liberty Lobbyists, they may know their history too well. This is not the Augustan Age. It is the nuclear age, and the country's real enemies are rocket-rattlers, not robber barons. A national leader who tackled today's problems with the all-or-nothing gusto of a Roosevelt could wind up with literally nothing — no life, no nation. Kennedy must speak softly, for he carries the biggest stick of all time. In Blacklett Strait after the crash of PT-109 he told his drenched crew, "There's nothing in the book about a situation like this." Nor is there now. His generation is writing its own primer, the first lesson of which is patience. Icy antagonists must be dealt with icily. "Khrushchev," Larry O'Brien observes wryly, "has some unusual advantages as a politician." Countering these advantages requires exceptional qualities, and one of them may be the President's poise. Perhaps this is the new courage, and his the first profile in it. A sedulous poise can be deceptive. That 3 A.M. mote of light in the mansion's third-floor rear is there because his involvement is total. Only do not expect him to mount a rostrum the next day and break out a crying towel. It is highly improbable that he will talk to you about it if you ask. Inquire about his insomnia and he changes the subject. Mention the burdens of office and he turns aside with a light understatement: "I have a nice home, the office is close by, and the pay is good."

The home — his and America's fifty million others — is, of course, the point of the thing; certainly there is no other excuse for the arms insanity. In the White House bromides about the wife and kids sound less absurd. "Let's do this for Jack, for Jackie, and for Caroline," was the rallying cry of O'Brien's Hill scouts in the Eighty-seventh's first session. It became a joke. The notion that Jack and Jackie needed anything was entertaining, and the political possibilities of baby-kissing had been exhausted some time ago. Yet aversion for corn obscures the patent fact that without the Carolines, nuclear age tension would be not only unbearable, but somewhat pointless. "It doesn't really matter as far as you and I are concerned," John Kennedy confided to an intimate after his futile attempt to stare Khrushchev down in Vienna. "What really matters is the children." Obviously the whole works, if it does work, is working for them, and their ignorance of the hows and whys merely makes the task more poignant.

The First Family's first child treats the panoply of office with innocent irreverence. Without understanding what the Presidency is, she is for it. One autumn day when hurricane warnings were posted the Kennedys evacuated Hyannis Port for a nearby camp, and Caroline raced around asking whether anyone wanted to ride "in a *White House* car," knowing that, for some strange reason, the phrase would impress adults. It would be stretching to call her a typical little girl — the typical child does not remark, as Caroline did when she spotted a costumed figure on a liquor label, "Oh, there's Louis Quatorze!" — but that was a sign of her mother's membership in the Quality, not of her father's job. Swank aside, she seems normal enough to most people. There is an exception. "Caroline," Joe Kennedy told me earnestly, "is a genius," and his judgment was not, he insisted, influenced by the fact that she happened to be his granddaughter. After the hurricane blew out to sea he took her and her Welsh terrier Charley for a two-and-a-half-hour boat ride. They talked all the time, and the ambassador regarded it as an extremely interesting conversation, a real exchange of views. At one point they discussed Charley's character. She spoke at some length about the ways of dogs, and Joe listened, rapt, as though she were Albert Payson Terhune.

The President is answerable for much of the public interest in his daughter. At 6:45 P.M. on Hyannis Port Saturdays, for example, he hoists her and her peers aboard his motorized golf cart and convoys his squealing passengers to a candy store four blocks away. Being in the driver's seat, he could discourage press coverage of the ritual. He doesn't. He has a hunch his daughter enjoys the attention, and he knows he does. Such diversions were impossible for Senator Kennedy, because he wasn't around. Being Chief Executive has brought him an unexpected bonus: he is much closer to his family. Caroline's mother likes that part. "Jackie thought the Presidency would hurt their marriage," one of the couple's oldest friends says, "and she has been surprised and pleased to find that it's the other way around." From her sitting room window in the mansion proper she can and occasionally does look down on the rose garden and the French windows of his office. Jacqueline rarely intrudes in the West Wing, though after watching the successful retrieval of John Glenn over the sitting room's television set she did dart downstairs, race along the outdoor portico, and burst in on her husband, quivering with excitement.

Caroline makes the trip more often. Frequently she wanders over just to say hello. If he is busy she can chat with Mrs. Lincoln, and she doesn't mind. She sees so much of him elsewhere these days. Mornings she watches him shave with his safety razor and talks to him while he bathes. Her mother has always read to her; now he does, too, explaining the adventure of Goldilocks, the forgetfulness of Bo-peep, and the London Bridge disaster, together with assorted animal tales. As a scholar he prefers a child's version of the *Iliad* and the *Odyssey*, and as an author he likes to spin tales of his own, although, like many another father, he sometimes buckles under the demand for new material and resorts to literary piracy. One of Caroline's favorites is a sea story. He has embroidered it a great deal, and by now it would make a pretty fair novel. The chief character is a one-legged sea captain who pursues a white whale.

Looking around him the President says, "I was away every weekend for three years." He smiles slightly and adds, with the air of the sailor home from the sea and the hunter home from the Hill, "Now I've settled down." Caroline literally believes this — certain politicians will be startled to learn that she thinks of the Executive Mansion as a permanent Kennedy acquisition — and certainly her father's new routine suggests that of a man striking root. He habitually smokes one or two cigars every day, eats lunch regularly for the first time since childhood, and has put on ten pounds. The weight is largely a tribute to a superb chef his wife hired in New York. It is also something of a problem, because it all goes to his jowls. On television the effect would be singular, so four days before a major speech he goes on a crash diet. That ascetic expression on your screen is partly illusion. The man is simply starved.

He doesn't diet for vanity's sake. The sudden appearance of a puffy Chief Executive might unsettle the nation, and today a President must think of such things. The time has passed when a William Howard Taft could regularly get himself wedged in a White House bathtub and howl to be extricated. Embassies would howl back if there were such incidents now. Cartoons would be drawn in Amsterdam and Bombay; editorials would be written, prestige reevaluated. Most of the people for whom the President is responsible have never seen him — entire nations are ineligible to vote for him — yet they feel his impact all the same. "When he creaks they groan," wrote Sidney Hyman. "When he wobbles they feel unhinged." The many cables Jacqueline Kennedy has received from French towns laying claim to her Bouvier ancestry are not a tribute to her Gallic charm; de Gaulle *gloire* notwithstanding, Frenchmen know that Jacqueline's husband has almost as much to say about the future of their country as Marianne's guardian. "The President of the United States," writes David Butler, of Oxford, "is the President of Britain. However closely the British guard their independence, however scrupulously the President respects it, he still makes decisions that are more important to their fate than any made by the Prime Minister."

His every act is significant to someone. In the era of the Zoomar lens, even the details of his personal life assume ludicrous importance. Let him decline a Homburg, and a segment of the economy shudders. Let him reach for a cigar, a glass of milk, a rocking chair — or the *Iliad* — and other segments feel braced. If he signs documents with Estabrook pens,

Parker pens must be presented to visiting children. The very temperature on his thermometer can influence stock exchanges; whenever he appears in bad weather without a hat his tailor gets complaining letters. The President is being watched all the time. If he grew fat, developed a tic, or began to speak with a stammer, there would be repercussions.

For while the world has changed, the Presidency is essentially unchanged. It is still a very personal office. Only one man can hold it. From a distance it tends to merge with the entire executive branch; its powers seem to be divided among the faceless members of a team. In crises this comforts those to whom facelessness and anonymity suggest impersonal precision. They delude themselves. Sitting with the President, one's most vivid perception is of the man's solitude, followed by a realization of why, for most voters, the White House hasn't much to do with conventional politics. Politics puts a man there, and helps him get the job done, but he cannot be a true chief unless we, and he, know when to forget party loyalties. He and his understudy are the sole men for whom we all vote. Without a President there could be no United States.

President Kennedy gives his various publics varied impressions. Diverse observers see him playing left field, right field, center field, all fields — carrying a red flag, a black flag, or no flag at all. This variety may arise from the complexity of the man. Really he is many men. He is a patrician and a politician;

he is both a field commander and a scholar. He shuns emotional displays. Yet he is moved by poverty, and when he is crossed he is a Tartar. He is jocose, but under the façade there is, though scarcely suspected, a dark vein of sadness. Although he is astonishingly candid, no one can keep a secret better. Despite his intellectualism, he is disdainful of academics. Despite his disdain for reformers, he has a vision of, and a plan for, global freedom. Statesmen who have spurned the mob stimulate him, but no President has cultivated the crowd so assiduously, and in him introversion and extroversion coexist.

He is not all things to all men. Among the labels which do not fit him are hotspur, demagogue, zealot. Dramatic breaks with tradition do not tempt him. He lives in a nation of bland change, of hueless progress, of silent, automated engines that move society almost without society's knowledge. His loyalty to his generation may be stronger than his loyalty to any other group. In America this is an age without passion for political novelty, and he acts his age. Nevertheless, he himself is not phlegmatic. Indeed, his most striking trait is his stamina. It has borne him through sickness and catastrophe. It won him the great prize, and with it he will be driven to close the Russian gap. He is the second son of a proud father, he survived to be first, and under certain circumstances survival itself can set a man apart.

That father is among the President's publics now, observing him with the rest of us. Unlike the haberdasher's correspondents, he doesn't fret about the weather. "I see him on TV, in rain and cold, bareheaded — and I don't worry," Joe Kennedy said as the opening year of the new Administration drew to a close. "I know nothing can happen to him. I tell you, something's watching out for him. I've stood by his deathbed four times. Each time I said good-by to him, and he always came back. In that respect he *is* like F.D.R. Because F.D.R. went to the edge, and he came back, too. And afterward he was unique. It's the same thing with Jack. You can't put your finger on it, but there's that difference. When you've been through something like that back, and the Pacific, what can hurt you? Who's going to scare you?"

Visiting Ted Kennedy's Senate campaign headquarters at 122 Bowdoin Street, Boston, this writer was shown certain wartime relics which had been overlooked by the President. The setting was anomalous: a dark, third-floor closet. The contents of the closet were a hodgepodge thrust aside to make space for the youngest Kennedy's politicking. Most of the odds and ends were trivia, but some were historic. Piled on a shelf were the late Joseph P. Kennedy, Jr.'s lawbooks, later used by Bobby and Ted. Below them, on another shelf, lay John Kennedy's Navy sword. And on a wire hanger in the back was the President's World War II dress blue uniform. The two rows of ribbons were upside down, the tailoring lacked H. Harris & Co.'s touch. Yet the nap was still stiff from the cleaner's iron, and the distinctive boxer's silhouette was familiar. The jacket had been hanging there a long time, its braid tarnishing, its ribbons begging readjustment. But Ted's pols, toiling away in the next room to the accompaniment of piped music, left it undisturbed. No one tried it on, of course. Somehow that would have been improper.

Besides, it wouldn't have fitted any of them.